4 MILLION REASONS TO CARE

How Your Church Can Help the Unemployed

D1798748

4 MILLION REASONS TO CARE

How Your Church Can Help the Unemployed

by
Peter Elsom
and
David Porter

MARC Europe
Church Action with the Unemployed

Elsom, Peter
    4 million reasons to care : how your church can help the unemployed.
    1. Church work with the unemployed—Great Britain
    I. Title   II. Porter, David, *1945*–
    331.13′7941′024362   BV2695.U64

    ISBN 0–947697–14–4

MARC is an integral part of World Vision, an international Christian humanitarian organisation. MARC's object is to assist Christian leaders with factual information, surveys, management skills, strategic planning and other tools for evangelism. MARC also publishes and distributes related books on mission, church growth, management, spiritual maturity, and other topics.

CAWTU (Church Action with the Unemployed) was established in 1981 to help and encourage local churches to work with unemployed people. It is ecumenical, supported by leaders of all the main churches. CAWTU identifies projects already established by local churches, launches new pilot projects, and produces leaflets, books, videos, and a newspaper, disseminating information about what has been and can be done. Fifty regional resource people have been appointed to advise how and where action is possible.

Contents

INTRODUCTION 1

PART 1: PERSPECTIVES
What is work? Some biblical guidelines 6
  A creation ordinance
  Work and dignity
  Work and social responsibility
The roots of the problem: a historical overview 9
  The Twenties and Thirties
  Beveridge and Keynes
  The beginnings of decline
  The effect on work security
  Devaluation and its aftermath
  Soaring unemployment
  The Social Contract
  Radical departures
  Current policies
  The challenge
  Alternative models

PART 2: SOME COMMON MYTHS
Statistical uncertainty 27
  New ways of counting
  Seasonal adjustment
  The significance of the statistics
'It's all a matter of getting on your bike' 31
  Mobility
  Fragmenting structures
  Towards healthy communities
Technological unemployment 35
  The case against technology
  Technology and rising demand
  The wider benefits of technology
  The needs of the individual
The leisure industry solution 39
Long-term unemployment 41
  Long-term youth unemployment
  Long-term adult unemployment
Female employment and unemployment 49
Conclusion 53

PART 3: PROJECTS FOR ACTION
Introduction 55
  Biblical giving
Work Agencies 57
  Facts and figures
Pay cuts for jobs 61
  The Christian at work

Providing capital for new business ventures   65
  Loan guarantee
  Private lending
  A venture programme
The job saver scheme   70
  How businesses fail
  The stresses of failure
  The significance of cash
  Funding growth
  Giving help
Work sharing in a climate of de-manning   83
  The Job Splitting and Phased Retirement schemes
  Work sharing and new jobs
How to become a government agent   88
  Opportunities for volunteering
  The Youth Training Scheme
  The Community Programme
The pastoral support of the unemployed   96
  Work and the time dimension
  Work and authority
  Work and money
  Work and self-worth
  Unemployment and the time dimension
  Unemployment and authority
  Unemployment and money
  Unemployment and self-worth
  The call to pastoral love
  Counselling: the Church's role
  Examples of 'drop in' counselling centres
Job Exports   114
  The import factor
  Export by inertia
  Channels of communication
  Local opportunities in retail trouble-shooting
Co-operatives   119
  Finding out more
  The advantages of co-operatives
  Church involvement
The early retirement debate   124
  An Action in Retirement Centre
Church twinning   128

PART 4: HOW TO GET ORGANISED   131
  Getting the Facts
  Forming an unemployment action group

CONCLUSION: A CALL TO ACTION   139

  Notes   142

CAWTU   143

  Local CAWTU Contacts

  Names and Addresses of Helpful Organisations   146

LAMBETH PALACE, LONDON, SE1 7JU

September, 1985

Unemployment is a continuing scourge in our
society, inflicting pain and causing severe loss of
identity. It is frequently responsible for the break-up
of families and, indeed, of entire communities. The
division between those who have work and those who do
not casts a blight on the whole nation. Christians want
to know what practical steps they can take to change this,
and to introduce new life into a state of hopelessness and
despair.

Peter Elsom and David Porter explain why local
churches have a special responsibility to be informed and
involved. They illustrate what has already been done, and
make serious proposals for new action based on proven pilot
schemes.

I welcome the publication of this useful book,
and urge all readers to persuade their churches to accept
the challenge of the recommendations outlined in the
concluding chapter of this timely publication.

Archbishop of Canterbury

Acknowledgements

We would like to place on record our appreciation of all those people throughout the country who provided information about their experiences of working with unemployment action groups.

We are also deeply grateful to Elaine Cooper, who worked tirelessly typing innumerable drafts; and yet found time to read the text, offer advice, and above all give us encouragement.

Introduction

by David Porter

In Birkenhead, on Merseyside, there are human scavengers on Bidston Moss rubbish tip.

They are the unemployed.

They move purposefully among the rubbish and dirt, scrutinising what they find, in search of anything that might be of some use and save money.

Like most new sociological patterns in the north of England, this phenomenon has attracted its quota of researchers and academics who have written articles about the scavengers, their origins, behaviour and attitudes.

So – like most new sociological patterns – it has inserted a comfortable paper buffer between the armchair reader and the bleak, litter-strewn heaps in Birkenhead and other towns and cities.

But nothing can buffer the unprepared reader for the first sight of photographs such as those which appeared briefly in the media in the summer of 1985, showing men and women and children picking through the garbage that the rest of us have thrown out. The shock value of the image has been well understood by the media; a Yorkshire Television programme on unemployment in August 1985 used footage of the Bidston scavengers to open the programme, though the cases discussed in what followed were all located far away from Birkenhead.

It really is a new development.

I grew up on Merseyside, and when I moved into a flat in Liverpool's Toxteth I joined in the local pastime of inspecting every rubbish skip I saw and glancing at every Corporation dump, in case somebody had thrown out something that was either still useful or still attractive.

In Amsterdam too I have often seen that useful neighbourliness whereby one family, trying to fit a new item of furniture into an already crowded apartment, will leave a perfectly useable piece on the pavement, knowing that some passer-by will snap it up within the day.

Even now, living in a village in one of the wealthier parts of Hampshire (though admittedly less prosperously than some of our neighbours) – several light-years away, in employment terms, from Toxteth – our family has a sturdy bench in our garden bought from an entrepreneur who had set up business on the local Council tip, picking out saleable rubbish as it was dumped and selling it to those who came later.

Scavenging is, in that pleasant sense, a national sport. But on Merseyside it is totally different. It is sheer necessity. The difference is the difference between hitch-hiking for fun, and hitch-hiking because you really have no other way to travel.

Thinking about unemployment has traditionally been something of a problem for the Christian. It is often difficult to sort out cultural preconceptions from the biblical framework.

Where, for example, does it say in the Bible that a person has to earn more than he needs to provide for his family properly, cover his outgoings, and prevent him from being an avoidable burden on others? Yet for many Christians, a high salary and a position of seniority and influence are thought to be in some way connected with God's ideal for his people.

Or where does it say in Scripture that a manual job is less worthy than a managerial, academic or professional one? Yet for some perfectly sincere Christians there is something unbiblical in not going to university, despite the fact that for centuries, a university education was outside the reach of most of Christendom.

It's hard to break free from the concept which we have inherited as part of the Protestant work ethic – that who we are is defined by the work we do. But we must break free of it, because if we do not we have no option but to regard the unemployed in our society and in our churches as less than whole people.

And yet unemployment is a lacerating and repellent experience for those who witness it and those who suffer it. We begin this book with a reference to the Merseyside scavengers because one of the most obvious casualties in unemployment is human dignity. The London suburbanite who has just discovered a Victorian chest of drawers in a local skip will boast of it gleefully in the pub that night. The unemployed person who is scavenging in hopes of finding some needed piece of furniture that he or she can never hope to pay for out of the dole doesn't talk about it. There is little to take pleasure in, and nothing to take pride in.

We write out of the conviction that unemployment is profoundly hated by the vast majority of those who experience it.

That might hardly need stating. But it is astonishing and depressing to find so many Christians who today will in all seriousness argue that there are plenty of jobs available, and that the unemployed are not really trying.

Others, from the security (illusory though that might often be) of well-paid, interesting and stimulating jobs of their own choosing, will deliver dismissive judgements on the unemployed for not gratefully snapping up jobs which are clearly unsuitable, either because the person in question is incapable of doing them or because the job would in no way solve the problem (such as a short-term job which paid much less than the dole and had hours which effectively prevented the person taking it from pursuing long-term employment).

So this book is written in the assumption that unemployment is a social evil of large and increasing proportions. Our title is drawn from the fact that in real terms the number of unemployed in British society today approaches four million. Viewed in terms of a percentage of the total adult population, that is in itself an alarming figure but it is really meaningless. The figures which shockingly demand action are those relating to specific areas, such as the city of Liverpool, where among under 25-year olds the unemployment figure at the beginning of 1984 stood at 42% and that among adults at almost 26%.[1]

In practical terms that means that every fourth adult you see in Liverpool, statistically speaking, has no job; and that one out of every two school-leavers will almost certainly face long-term unemployment.

But the statistics are averages, and conceal even worse

realities. The percentages change even between different schools. There are schools in Liverpool where most pupils will find some sort of job; there are others where hardly any will. Whole areas of the city have most of a generation unemployed, with consequent social and personal problems.

And the pattern can be seen in many other areas of Britain; Liverpool is by no means unique.

Faced with a problem as serious as this, and with all the problems that derive from it, Christians cannot opt out. There is no biblical position which allows us to sit back and let the government – any government – solve the problem as best it can. The problem of unemployment is already to be seen in our churches and in the neighbourhoods where those churches are called to witness.

In this book, we examine what can be done, give examples of what is being done, and also present some new ideas.

Any book that carries two names on the title page demands some explanation of exactly who has done what.

Both of us are self-employed in different capacities. I am a full-time writer and editor, and Peter Elsom is a management consultant with a long experience in employment agency management and in distribution and manufacturing.

The book arises out of many hours of discussions and research, primarily concerned to create new job opportunities and to encourage other Christians to think similarly. In counselling and talking with unemployed people over a period of several years we have both been convinced of the need for a genuinely radical rethinking by the Church to deal with unemployment.

We have also both been unemployed and in receipt of Social Security benefit for varying periods of time. Though these periods were not very long (my own most substantial unemployed stretch was seven months), it does at least mean that we have had some experience of the emotional and spiritual implications of unemployment and have gone through the dreary rituals of 'signing-on'. At least we know that UB-40 isn't just a pop group. We know first-hand, if in only a limited way, that unemployment hurts.

The main author of the book is Peter Elsom, and the main arguments of the book are his. Wherever we speak in the first person, the statements, experiences cited and opinions are Peter's. I have acted as a sounding-board, contributed some ideas of my own, and in some cases have suggested changes of approach and emphasis. We both subscribe equally to the practical, sociological and theological statements made in this book and take joint responsibility for its contents.

The initial synopsis was hammered out by Peter, by me, and by Tony Collins of MARC Europe. Peter and I have shared the actual writing of the book approximately equally, and I have been responsible for the final revisions, editing and presentation.

We have been given a great deal of help by many organisations and individuals, and a full list of acknowledgements is given elsewhere. Any shortcomings in the book are the responsibility of Peter and myself, not of those who have helped us.

We would like to dedicate this book to Rachel Stear and Martin Hines, with whom we have discussed many of the subjects in this book over several years; and above all, to our long-suffering wives, Daphne and Tricia.

David Porter
August 1985

Part 1: Perspectives

There is no doubt at all that unemployment is one of today's major social problems. But how did it become so, and when? Why is it that Britain appears to have a much more serious problem than many of her competitors? And what does the Bible have to say about work?

We begin with a brief overview of some biblical principles concerning the nature of work. Then we look at unemployment in the light of recent history, to set the problem in its historical context.

What is work? Some biblical guidelines

As with many similar subjects, we will understand the Bible's teaching on the meaning of work if we consider the Bible as a whole rather than relying on isolated proof-texts. When we do this, we find that its teaching on this subject is very straightforward.

Work, according to Scripture, is a gift from God. When we have no work, we are deprived of something that he wants us to have for our enjoyment, benefit and fulfilment, both as individuals and as members of society.

This biblical view of work is quite different from, for example, that which sees work as a drudgery, part of the fall of man. Those who argue this sometimes quote Genesis 3:17–19 to support their case:

> Cursed is the ground because of you; through painful toil you will eat of it all the days of your life . . . By the sweat of your brow you will eat your food.

But work did not begin with the Fall. It was part of the original good creation of God.

A creation ordinance

In the opening verses of the Bible, God is described as actively carrying out a programme of work. Day by day, he added to the world he was creating. It might seem strange to talk of God, who is all-powerful, as working; but that is exactly how the Bible describes it; moreover, he had need of rest afterwards:

> By the seventh day God had finished the work he had been doing; so on the seventh day he rested from all his work. And God blessed the seventh day and made it holy, because on it he rested from all the work of creating that he had done.
>
> (Genesis 2:2–3)

Earlier, man has been described as made in God's image (1:28). So it is not surprising to find Adam, who bears the likeness of a working God, given work for himself: the tending of his own home, the Garden of Eden (2:15).

If human work were a drudge, it would be strange indeed to find it among the provisions that God makes for Adam and Eve (who in verse 18 is described as a 'helper' – she is a co-worker). But work is one of the many good things in Eden. It is one of the responsibilities and privileges of being made in the image of God, of being the governor of the Garden. Significantly, when the serpent creates a mood of resentment in Eve, it is not about the existence of work that she complains. Drudgery entered into the world at the Fall, not at the creation. At the Fall, work ceased from being a pure joy and delight to mankind. Toil and exploitation became possible (for example, Exodus 1:11–14), and also the use of work for self-glorification (Ecclesiastes 2:4–11; Luke 12:16–22).

Work and dignity

Yet throughout history, man's work has remained, at least potentially, part of his likeness to God. And being like God in our work does not necessarily mean being the managing director of a company, or the international director of a multi-national corporation. When God himself lived on this earth as a man in the person of Jesus, he worked as a carpenter (Mark 6:3); Paul the apostle, whose missionary work was the main force in the building of the Early Church, worked as a tent maker (Acts 18:3).

Sometimes it has been argued that work is a necessary evil, to be got through somehow. But far from being so, it is part of man's dignity and a measure of his worth; even the worker least respected in the eyes of men has the dignity to which his labour entitles him; the labourer is worthy of his hire (Luke 10:7). Seen in this light, to remove a man's work is to remove a part of his self-worth.

Even the Preacher in Ecclesiastes, with his prevailing pessimism, reaches a positive view of work: 'So I saw that there is nothing better for a man than to enjoy his work, because that is his lot' (Ecclesiastes 3:22).

Work and social responsibility

In the Bible, work is described as something that gives dignity to the individual and also benefit to the community. As such it is part of service, which for the Christian can never be merely service to other people but also part of his obedience to Jesus Christ; this is made clear in such passages as Paul's advice to slaves:

> Slaves, obey your earthly masters with respect and fear, and with sincerity of heart, just as you would obey Christ. Obey them not only to win their favour when their eye is on you, but like slaves of Christ, doing the will of God from your heart. Serve wholeheartedly, as if you were serving the Lord, not men, because you know that the Lord will reward everyone for whatever good he does, whether he is slave or free.
>
> (Ephesians 6:5–7)

In this, a Christian is simply following Jesus, who said to his disciples, 'I am among you as one who serves' (Luke 22:27).

In the light of that pattern of service, the biblical warnings against idleness acquire added importance. In 1 Thessalonians 5:14, Paul's instruction is 'Warn those who are idle'. In 2 Thessalonians 3:6, the injunction is stronger: 'Keep away from every brother who is idle and does not live according to the teaching you received from us'. Paul also stresses that by means of work, it is possible to help the disadvantaged in society; the converted thief is urged to 'work, doing something useful with his own hands, that he may have something to share with those in need' (Ephesians 4:28).

We shall be making reference to the biblical teaching on work throughout this book. But even in this brief overview, we can see that for men and women work is, according to Scripture, something that belongs not to their Fall but to their glory as image-bearers of God; a way of having dignity and asserting their self-worth; and a way of serving other people.

The Bible does not say that one's work is the sum total of one's worth; and it does not say that the only work worthy of the name is that which carries a wage-packet with it. But in our society, the reality of losing, or never having, paid employment is that any work after a time becomes impossible. In the grim reality of life on the dole, endless job-application rejections and social stereotyping by the media (and, all too often, by the employed), the individual's dignity and opportunities for service are early casualties.

The roots of the problem: a historical overview

The beginnings of the present unemployment crisis go back many years. To properly understand it, we must view it in the perspective of recent history.

Successive governments have claimed – with justification – that unemployment is not just a British disease. It is a world-wide phenomenon. Any realistic evaluation of the global economic situation today has to take into account the effect of the unemployment factor.

But why is it that the United Kingdom, which seems to have so many advantages (like North Sea Oil and near self-sufficiency in several consumer markets), has had employment problems on such a dramatic scale?

In this section we will examine some of the reasons, because the relief of unemployment – as with any chronic disease – is best achieved when one knows the original symptoms and the circumstances that brought them about. Thinking about the causes of our present problems is a useful reminder also of a fact which on its own should make us search for remedies: that in the case of the unemployed, as with most minority groups, those affected are often the least responsible for the situation.

The Twenties and the Thirties

A good place to begin is the interwar period, with the economic boom that followed the First World War. Such was the national optimism by 1920 that unemployment insurance was extended to cover almost everybody who was in employment. It was never thought that the scheme might have to do anything more than provide assistance to individuals who happened to be experiencing short-term unemployment.

But the euphoria was short-lived. The unemployment figures began to creep up. There was a national sense of disillusionment. The country had survived – and won – a great war; the post-war rejoicings had been matched by a period of relative prosperity. So why, it was asked, was that prosperity threatened by rising unemployment and a declining economic growth? Many of the British people at that time felt cheated out of a prosperity to which their sufferings had entitled them.

The feeling that they had been duped was aggravated as disaster followed disaster. In 1926 came the General Strike. In 1931 the National Economy Act was passed, effectively reversing the economic gains of the post-war decade and reducing benefits. Rigorous means-testing followed. In Jarrow, two-thirds of the population became unemployed. The 'hunger marches' of that time have passed into the history books. Parts of South Wales experienced 50% unemployment. Lack of food and clothing was the rule rather than the exception.

Barely fifty years later, it is difficult to realise the circumstances in which many people lived. The hated Poor Laws, instituted in the reign of Elizabeth I, were only amended in 1834 when the New Poor Law was passed – which arguably made life much harder for the poor anyway, as it introduced workhouses. Health insurance on a minor scale was only introduced in 1911. The England of Dickens was well within living memory for many of the population.

Such a catastrophic reversal of fortunes induced a profound national psychological shock. It was a time of job insecurity, unemployment, social division, lack of social welfare provision, and a very real sense of despair. The reverberations continue to be felt in our own day, not least because these factors played a crucial part in establishing priorities and shaping the economic policies adopted after 1945.

After the Second World War the nation and its leaders had the grim lesson of the Thirties behind them. There was an over-riding concern that such a tragedy should never happen again.

Beveridge and Keynes

This mood of determination and new beginnings found expression in one of the charter documents of the Welfare State: the Beveridge Report of 1944, *Full Employment in a Free Society*. The vision of Beveridge – the architect of our Social Security system and one of the great reformers of the twentieth century – was to put right the legacy of the social ills of the Thirties.

At that time also John Maynard Keynes was propounding his theory of Demand Management, which argued that government spending could act as a safety valve for market-place demand. The result would be to even out the fluctuations and cyclical effects of market economy. The theory was that a government really committed to full employment could achieve it by adjusting its spending appropriately. After the horrors of the Depression and the rigour of the Thirties, politicians and electorate alike joyfully pounced on this concept. Many saw it as the remedy for all the problems of the Twenties and Thirties. The 1944 Employment

White Paper was passed unanimously.

It did not go as far as Beveridge had hoped. But it did commit itself to 'the maintenance of a high and stable level of employment after the war'.

Beveridge was deeply influenced by Keynesian theory. In his report he stated:

> It must be the function of the State in future to ensure adequate total outlay, and by consequence to protect its citizens against mass unemployment, as definitely as it is now the function of the state to defend the citizens against attack from abroad and against robbery and violence at home.[1]

Without doubt the goal of relative full employment was achieved during the twenty years following the war. But what *is* in doubt is the extent to which this was achieved by demand management policies.

During this period the policies pursued were not by present-day standards particularly expansionary; a major constraint on the government, for example, was the 'Bretton Woods' system of fixed exchange rates. This tied the pound to a dollar standard.

The beginnings of decline

Since the free enterprise, young economy of the USA was committed to inflation control, there was little scope for injecting high demand into the United Kingdom. Virtually nothing was done to restimulate demand. Even so, the natural level of post-war demand was very high. Consumer goods, unavailable during the war years, were eagerly demanded by a luxury-starved society. The massive expenditure directed to the war effort could now be redirected to the commercial development of consumer goods, and to the necessary intensive rebuilding programme. Indeed, during this period relatively full employment was maintained with unemployment running at an average of only 1.5%.

But despite this period of relative economic tranquillity,

Britain was already starting to fall behind its major economic competitors. From 1948 to 1958, annual percentage growth rates in the United Kingdom were only 3%. During the same period Germany achieved 14.5%, France 6.4%, and Italy 8.7%. The six countries of the Common Market of that time achieved 9%. Worse, our annual growth rate in prices and wages – 4.6% – was beginning to head the European league. The corresponding figure for Germany was 1.6%, for Italy 2.8%, for the EEC 3.6%, and for France (a worse figure than our own) 7.4%.

These statistics are striking enough in themselves, but when one considers the high share that the United Kingdom had of world exports of manufactured goods they are all the more surprising. And they demonstrate the beginnings of a decline over which no one political party presided; the Conservative Party held office 1935–45, the Labour Party 1945–50 and 1950–1, and the Conservatives again 1951–5.

The effect on work security

It was perhaps during this period of world prosperity, fed by the idea that government needed only to create demand to generate jobs and that no other factor was a threat to a good standard of living, that the concept of 'the world owing one a living' first took shape amongst some in Britain. The security of virtual full employment blunted the sharp-edged, self-determining Protestant work ethic which had been the stimulus and driving force for much of the prosperity of the Victorian era. The mood was well caught in Harold Macmillan's classic phrase, 'You've never had it so good'.

But in reality, Britain was losing in a competitive world. As this was gradually realised, there was mounting pressure to devalue the pound; and those pressures, together with high-growth ambitions aimed to fund a large increase in the Welfare programme, meant that in mid-1966 (for the first time since 1945) a major package of restrictive measures was introduced. It included a freeze on wages.

The measures were designed to restore world confidence in the pound. But the domestic effect was that the work force in

Britain, shocked by the situation and by what seemed to be a radical change in fortunes, expressed their need for greater work security by joining Trade Unions in much greater numbers and making their voices heard by industrial stoppages. Again, the statistics make the point clearly: the number of working days (in thousands) lost through industrial action in 1950 were 1,334; in 1960, 3,024; by 1970, 10,980. Perhaps for the government of the day the most memorable action was the Seamen's Strike of 1966, which had a major effect on exports, lasted for six and a half weeks, and came right in the middle of a pound crisis. We now know that the effect of the strike on the pound was disastrous.

Devaluation and its aftermath

As British prices grew less competitive, Britain's deliveries more unreliable and its deteriorating industrial relations more publicised, our traditional world markets took note and voted with their orders. The balance of payments continued to decline. Unemployment rose to a record 2.3% (over 500,000). In November 1967 the battered pound was finally devalued by 14.3% – to the accompaniment of the revealing assurance, 'The pound in your pocket is worth the same as before'.

But it wasn't, although devaluation in terms of price-competitiveness of our products resulted, with better control of government expenditure in the evening-out of unemployment to 547,000 (2.4%) in 1968, and by 1970 to 577,000 (2.5%).

There was another result of devaluation. The heyday of the sixties was well past, and the price of imported goods was rising sharply. The pound in your pocket would simply not buy as many imported goods as before.

Thus the 'inflation spiral' gathered momentum. During this period power shifted to the Unions, aided notably by the increased Unionisation of the public sector. Most government expenditure had been in the public sector. The Keynesian balance between spending and demand was therefore at risk, and by 1970 annual inflation had reached 8%.

The 'In Place of Strife' legislation was an attempt to create a balance of co-operation, depending upon the Unions maintaining high-level control of their membership and with government working out a policy of wage restraint. That policy would then be imposed by the Unions on their members. But despite these efforts earnings continued to rise, from 7% in 1968 to 14% in 1970.

These developments in the United Kingdom were taking place against the backdrop of an increasing US influence in world affairs. The American economy was under stress from the demands of funding the Vietnam war and President Johnson's social programmes. The result was inflation of the economy, and that in turn affected the rest of the world.

Soaring unemployment

All this time, the British economy was tied to the dollar standard, but this was increasingly under pressure. Eventually in 1971 it collapsed, and a new era began – the era of floating exchange rates.

Still operating within the framework of Keynesian economics, the government of the day saw the opportunity of creating demand unencumbered by exchange controls. When in 1971 unemployment reached the million mark, a major drive for growth gathered momentum. The strategy adopted against inflation was a combination of a strict incomes policy with increased government spending.

But by now the Unions had become experienced in wage bargaining in inflationary times. They had seen too many instances of wage increases successfully negotiated only to be overtaken by inflation. They were now anticipating it and its future effects, and as a result were negotiating for much higher increases.

Attempts to enforce the incomes policy by the Industrial Relations Act simply made negotiations more confrontational – a process which culminated in the 1974 Miners' Strike. But before that took place, the first oil crisis exploded, following the Yom Kippur War. And in other parts of the world other governments had also been adopting spending policies in order to encourage demand.

And so the inflation spiral in Britain cut loose, fuelled by high levels of government spending, rocketing oil prices and soaring wage settlements. By 1976 the crisis had reached massive proportions. Prices were rising by almost 30% per annum, and unemployment stood at 1.3 million.

The Social Contract

In the world exporting race in manufactured goods, Britain slumped from 18.2% of the total in 1958 to 8.4% in 1976. In the same period Germany increased its share from 18.5% to

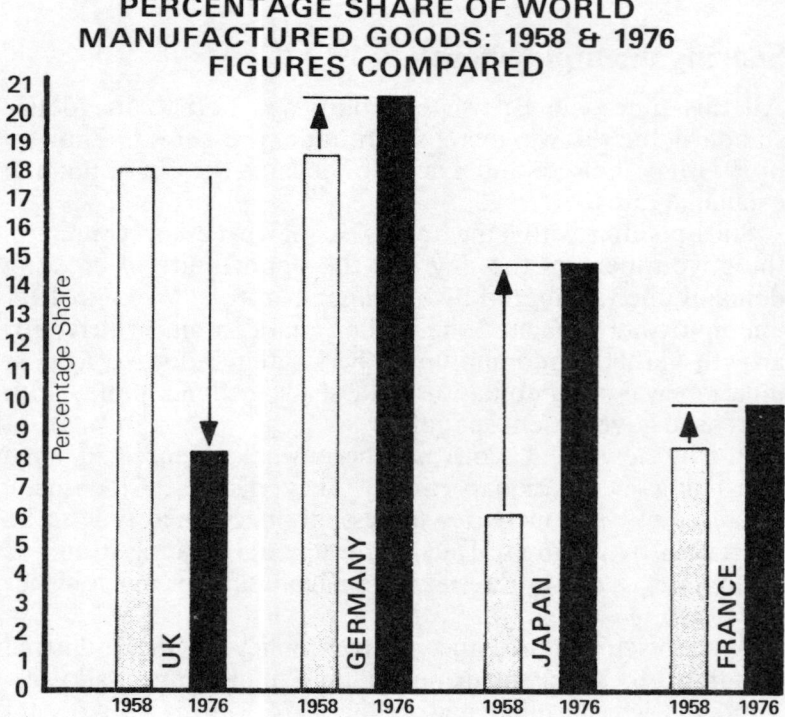

PERCENTAGE SHARE OF WORLD MANUFACTURED GOODS: 1958 & 1976 FIGURES COMPARED

20.6%, Japan from 6% to 14.7%, and France from 8.6% to 9.8%. But imports continued to rise, and as a result we faced a balance of payments deficit, made more difficult by the fact that industrial stoppages continued to increase.

Finally in 1976, with a rising oil import bill, worsening balances of payment and growing international indebtedness, the help of the International Monetary Fund was sought. The Fund imposed explicit monetary targets upon the government of the day, which involved savage cuts in government spending. In return they supplied a temporary loan. The 'Social Contract', which established voluntary wage restraint, had an immediate effect. During 1977–8 inflation dramatically dropped to single figures (approximately 8%), and unemployment remained relatively stable at 1.3 million.

But once again Britain was losing ground in world markets. The number of people involved in manufacturing – the 'index of industrial production' – reflected our failure to compete. Our productivity continued to decline. The Social Contract began to crack. When the pay round negotiations took place in 1978–9, the 'Winter of Discontent' was well established, and industrial action combined with inflationary wage settlements sent the industrial stoppage figures rocketing, and a vicious circle was set up in which the inflation rate was affected as well. At this time, unemployment actually came down to 1.24 million, reflecting in part the impact of the Social Contract. There was a further decline in productivity, however, indicating that part of the overall decline was due to overmanning.

Radical departures

Some sixty years after the starting point of our analysis, the new government in 1979 determined to apply a completely different set of policies. It abandoned the commitment to the 1944 White Paper and with it all that Keynes stood for. Instead it embarked upon a programme of monetarism, known as the Medium Term Financial Strategy. This set out to manage the economy by reducing the need for monetary growth and public sector borrowing, while at the same time promising to honour the Clegg Commission recommendations on comparability awards for public sector workers.

It was a difficult enough package in itself, but the climate of the 'Winter of Discontent' and the second oil crisis made it an impossible one. Sterling was by now viewed as a 'petro-currency', and this was a heavy strain on exchange rates. The combination of this and the tightening monetary policy put manufacturing industry under enormous pressure. A massive increase of VAT from 8% to 15% further reduced the demand for manufactured goods, and interest rates soared to a minimum lending rate (MLR) of 17% – which in its turn severely increased companies' costs. This and pay settlements at over 20%, dearer energy and sterling at $2.40 forced companies to search for ways of reducing costs in order to continue in business.

The government offered no lifeline, and the only option was to cut plant, machinery, stock, buildings, transport – and, of course, people. Many companies went to the wall. Many were taken over with a view to rationalisation. Almost all suffered severe cutbacks.

Within less than a year unemployment had doubled to over two million. By 1980, the UK Index of Industrial Production (based on a value of 100 for 1958) was only 159, compared with Germany at 254, France at 253, Italy at 361 and the six countries of the EEC at 269. The figures for numbers employed in manufacturing were equally depressing. Inflation shot back up to 20%. Industrial production actually declined 12% over 1979. Confrontation between government and unions inevitably followed. In 1979 an all-time record number of 29,474,000 working days were lost through stoppages, primarily in the engineering sector.

The government pursued a policy of increasing demand and incentive by cutting taxes. This gave the rich the biggest benefits, while the poorly paid and unemployed still had to find the money to pay for the VAT increases. The result was that demand was not significantly increased, manufacturing industries and the lower paid were hit, and the gap between rich and poor, the service industries of the south and the manufacturing industries of the north, became greater. Unemployment had its greatest impact in the north.

Such an extreme change in policies was in itself a recipe for polarisation, and this was seen in political life, in social

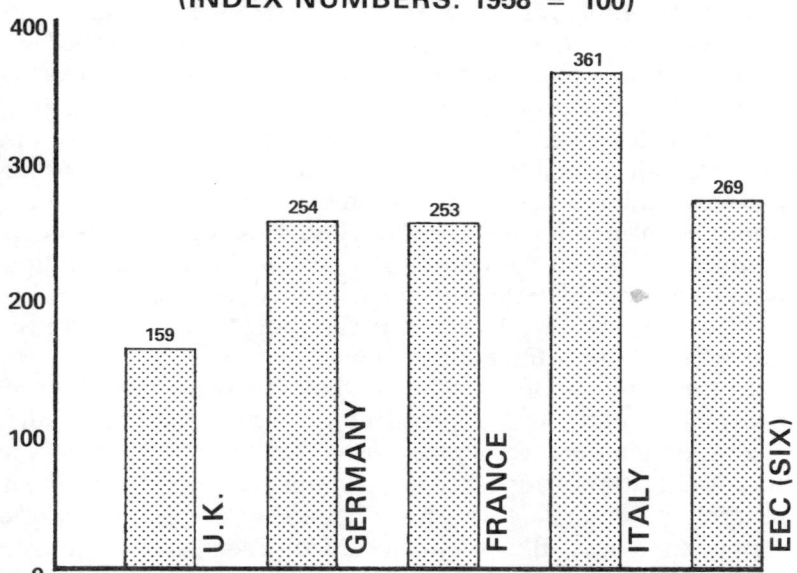

INDEX OF INDUSTRIAL PRODUCTION
(INDEX NUMBERS: 1958 = 100)

life, and particularly in management style.

Though it is true that the rest of the world, following the second oil crisis, was also in recession, few industrialised nations were as badly hit as the United Kingdom. Reacting to this situation the boardrooms of British industry took on a different style. The 'macho-management' of the overhead-choppers became the fashion; concentration on trimming down operations took the place of development, research, training, ways of stimulating demand and other priorities.

Current policies

This is the current philosophy; a belief that a slimmed-down, leaner United Kingdom, with increased productivity and a rate of inflation controlled at under 5%, will sooner or later win new markets and bring about economic growth. And with these, it is argued, employment will follow.

It may be so. There are intellectual arguments supporting

the present policy, and in the areas of inflation control and impact on some sectors of the world market, there are results to be seen. But even were one to concede the principle, the question that demands an answer is: how long will it take?

No economy can stand on its own in a competitive world. The deregulation of exchange controls and the current decline in demand for oil are beginning to have an effect. Manufacturing output has declined while our export of oil has increased, and the result has been that Britain has become a frequent net importer of manufactured goods. Our balance has only been maintained because of our oil exports. With a devaluing pound this should in the long term improve price competitiveness for exports, but the effect in the short term is to increase the prices of imported goods.

Commentators often indicate that the recession may be nearing its end, and a prospect of full order books and renewed high demand is put before us. But it is not so easy a solution as it may appear. Our manufacturing base has been severely eroded. Factories have been shut down. Sources of supply have been allowed to close. Contracts have been lost. Work forces have diminished beyond the point at which bringing them up to full strength is an easy matter. (To see a similar situation brought about by a very different set of circumstances one has only to consider the state of the British coal mines at the end of the 1984–5 Miners' Strike.)

To make matters worse, until recently the profitability of companies has been so low that investment to replace the plant jettisoned in 1979–80 has not happened to any great extent, and we are badly placed to respond to the opportunities now opening up for British industry as the recession begins to 'turn the corner'. As a result unemployment has continued to increase year by year until it stands today, by any method of counting, at over three million unemployed. The problem has not been helped by the population increases in the employable age range which will continue to affect the statistics until the end of the decade.

The history we have just examined might lead one to expect that our employment costs are declining as the size of the workforce declines. But they are not. In fact they continue to rise in comparison with our major competitors, and our share of world exports of manufactured goods continues to decline – by 8.2% in 1982. Despite major improvements our rate of inflation is higher than that of Japan or West Germany, and our productivity is still 5% less than that of our competitors. In theory, that means that at least 5% growth is essential, and due allowance made for the increase in the size of the population old enough to work, before the dole queues are reduced. And even the most optimistic of forecasters do not predict any major decline in the unemployment problem which in Britain is almost 50% more serious than in most of our major competitors. It is with us to stay.

The challenge

After such a long history of national and global influences, against which successive governments have struggled in vain, the individual reader might be excused for thinking that on his own he or she is totally powerless to do anything about the employment problem.

In fact the opposite is true. In this book we will be presenting many examples of ways in which individuals *can* make a difference, and the fact that they can bears out an essential truth: given that the present government is opposed to returning to Keynesian methods of increasing demand by public spending, and setting aside the rights and wrongs of such a policy, the fact remains that the country desperately needs a dramatic resurgence of entrepreneurial activity.

Business Week's 'International Report' of 16 July 1984 pointed out that seven out of every ten new jobs in America are created by entrepreneurs. That means that the growth of jobs in America is currently not generated by the big businesses, the multinationals, the major service industries or large-scale manufacturing systems. The growth is generated by individuals and small teams creating work and following through their ideas with help and backing from outside organisations and government.

Could it happen here?

It could. But there are several factors which make it more difficult.

The role of banking

Firstly, just as the interwar period established a pattern for later economic history, so in the same way it had a major effect on social attitudes to new businesses. The spirit of free enterprise was suppressed by the intense need for job security – which was taken to mean working for the government, or for large companies.

Secondly, and very significantly in terms of the capitalisation of small businesses, the Truck Act of 1831 (amended 1887) stated that employees had the right to be paid for their labour in coin of the realm. This meant that a high percentage of the population did not have bank accounts (and still do not).

The major developments in banking in recent years have placed the emphasis on increased efficiency of the banking system. Huge computerisation projects have been given higher priority than the stimulation of borrowing for new enterprises.

A system primarily designed to meet the needs of the 'banked population' and to maximise returns for shareholders tends to ensure a minimum of high-risk lending. Most of the 'new venture capital' has in the past few years been invested in organisations that already existed, rather than in the sort of 'one-man band' enterprise such as an individual applying for a loan of a few hundred pounds capital to start a window-cleaning business. Lending was traditionally heavily based upon the principle 'my word is my bond', and therefore the personality and credibility of the individual was scrutinised rather than the project being proposed. It must, however, be recognised that the clearing banks are lending their depositors' money; and traditional conservatism by these depositors has dictated low-risk lending.

It is only recently that the emphasis has begun to be placed on teaching the lending manager business skills which equip him to appraise a proposal properly. If the number of new business venture failures are anything to go by, the modern clearing bank manager still has much to learn.

Government loans

By the same token, the government loan scheme for those who

have few assets to support the borrowing has been a disaster. The number of failures has meant that such high interest rates are now required that the scheme is totally unacceptable as an overhead of most new businesses. The level of skill, in helping to advise and monitor progress not only at the outset but also when the business is established, is variable in the extreme. So a vicious circle is created; those who fail provide a further discouragement to others who might have been willing to try.

(American banking practice is quite different. Venture capital, to get entrepreneurs started in business, plays a major role. There are major equity markets which are very interested in high risk ventures, and deregulation together with technological changes have made this one of the most dynamic sectors of the US economy.)

In addition to these problems, most young people in Britain have been educated in a system designed to cater for the 'O' and 'A' Level student, with an appropriate academic bias. Few leave equipped to handle the practical issues of earning a living, let alone starting a business; and for the person who has been educationally unprepared, has never had a bank account, and possesses few assets, the opportunity to make his own way is minimal.

Often when somebody applies for a loan to start a small business, the first thing he is told to do is to find an accountant to appraise his project. This can be expensive, is sometimes unrealistic (as for example if the business proposed is a straightforward service project such as a taxi or gardening business), and does not provide an appraisal of the individual himself.

Attitudes to capitalisation

The historical background to this failure of commitment to high-risk venture projects goes back a long way. It is not a new problem. The hardest hit in the Depression were the working class, and during that time the Labour Party and the Unions recruited large numbers of members from that sector. This provided the dynamic for immediate post-war growth. But the concepts of security and a broader economic share-out based on a new programme of welfare and public ownership are radically different to programmes which depend upon entrepreneurial flair for much of their employment and growth of Gross National Product.

Historically, the see-saw of governments and policies as two ideologically opposed parties alternated in office did nothing to change the structure of British society, which remained endemically class-orientated. Indeed, it has produced further social, economic and political division. Consequently Britain today is fragmented on several levels, and is characterised by deep rifts. Management is isolated from the workforce, the house-owners from the non-house-owners, Tories from Labour. Categorisation of society habitually identifies capital with one fragment and labour with another; and very often, somebody who wants to start a new business is assumed to belong to a particular sector of society, while somebody who is unemployed is assumed to belong to another, different one. As a result it is often difficult for many people to imagine an unemployed person starting a new business.

Alternative models

This is an entirely false antithesis. There is no reason why capital and skills should be thought of as the prerogative of one political group or another. That this view is accepted at all is an indictment of the fragmentation and alienation of much of modern life.

Other countries provide other models. We have already considered America, the most entrepreneurial country in the world. In the USA, banking profits (as expressed in terms of return on capital) are lower than in Britain, but a constant flow of finance is generated for new ventures. The banks actively encourage this aspect of their business. Lenders are trained in the skills of business appraisal. The banking halls are inviting places, designed to attract the man in the street and totally undaunting. The lending manager and the borrower prepare cash flows together – so a learning process is set up; and, most important of all, the progress of the business is carefully monitored.

The difference in the US approach to entrepreneurs reflects a basic difference of philosophy between our two countries. Education is broadly based, and education beyond secondary schooling encouraged. The status of an individual is measured in terms of achievement, rather than birth or the nature of his employment. In the USA a new venture is described as exciting, in the true spirit of America. In Britain it is described as chancy, dangerous, courageous, a gamble; above all, lacking in security. Is it any wonder that the entrepreneurial spirit has been sleeping in the United Kingdom?

In Germany the 'working class' is thought of very highly, because of the contribution they make to the economy. They are often shareholders in the businesses that employ them, and are frequently involved in industrial decision-making. The educational system is intensely practical, with major emphasis on training for work and further on-the-job practical training.

In Japan, ventures are encouraged to succeed by a high level of support from banks and suppliers, with little regard to short-term losses and a strong emphasis on help and assistance in the early stages and assistance in planning one's way to success in the long term. As in Germany, the whole educational system is built around training for future employment, and is continued on into the work experience. All these differences of attitude and culture deeply affect the ability of a society to respond to economic difficulties, and they point to many of the problems presently facing Britain.

> The tale of soaring employment is the story of small business – the entrepreneur starting up a new company or the small businessman employing several dozen people. While national attention remains focused on the health of America's multinationals, job creation in the 1980s is increasingly the story of the little guy taking big risks.
>
> (*Business Week*, 'International Report',
> 16 July 1984.)

Perhaps the real heart of the problem is that of relating that attitude which is prevalent in the United States to the psychological problems of a society that has fought two world wars, lost an empire and suffered two major socio-economic disillusionments all within the space of the last seventy years.

Even the young people of today have spent much of their childhood in a period of relatively full employment, and had come to expect that they would share their parents' experience of leaving school, college or university and finding a job.

So the problems are not simply those of job creation and economic growth. They are also those of understanding the hurt, anger and fears that are implicit in the position in which the unemployed find themselves.

Part 2: Some Common Myths

For those who have not looked closely at recent employment history, the previous chapter may have exploded some myths. It is, for example, very easy to regard unemployment as a modern issue that has developed suddenly due to mismanagement by a particular government, group of Trade Unions, or sector of the workforce. If a sufficiently strong line were taken against the appropriate offender, or if there were a complete reversal of a particular set of political attitudes, then – it is sometimes argued – the problem would go away as quickly as it came.

But, as we have seen, it wouldn't. And there are many more myths currently circulating about unemployment which are just as misleading, which suggest unworkable solutions, and which, most tragically, have often determined attitudes to the unemployed people themselves which are unrealistic and judgemental.

In this section we intend to look at several of these misconceptions.

Statistical uncertainty

A good place to start is with the statistics themselves, which are a fertile breeding ground for misconceptions and preconceptions.

The main reason for this is that they are not only difficult to understand, but they often conflict with each other, depending on who has produced the figures and why.

Whenever a major disaster occurs, whether it be an air crash, a volcano erupting, or a serious fire, one of the most striking features is the media's conflict over the numbers of casualties involved. There is a similar lack of agreement in the compiling and interpreting of unemployment statistics.

We know that there must be an absolute figure somewhere. *Somebody* must know exactly how many people are unemployed. But nobody can tell us accurately what the figure is. The minute that the unemployment statistics are announced each month, a team of experts sets about explaining why a decrease is actually an increase, why the published figures omit a hundred and one other factors, and why – depending on where you are standing – the figures are really very good indeed or very bad indeed.

What follows is a simple description of how the published figures are calculated, and what their implications are in the total employment picture.

New ways of counting

When dealing with a series of statistics as complicated as those relating to unemployment, there are inevitably many factors which cannot be accurately quantified. For example: How many would not want to work even if they could? How many are unemployed but do not claim benefit? How many have not registered for work? How many are working in the 'black economy'?

Hence it is arguably just as important to establish consistent figures from which one can establish trends, as it is to know the actual numbers involved. If one can produce statistics which can reliably be said to bear some relationship to the unknown real figures, then it is possible to see whether the situation at a particular time is better or worse than that at a different period in the past. That question, of course, is of the greatest interest to government, economists and commentators.

But it is exactly at that point that the problem has been made very complicated. The government decided in principle to alter the basic way of measuring unemployment, most of the changes being made in October 1982.

The chief change was from using as a statistical base the numbers of people registered by the Job Centres who are seeking work, to counting the numbers of claimants at the Unemployment Benefit Offices. One advantage was that computerisation was made easier by this method – previously the count had been done manually – and there was consequently less delay between people finding jobs and the appropriate changes appearing in local and national statistics.

However, the changes introduced new inaccuracies. Since the 1983 Budget, men over sixty years old can secure National Insurance benefits without having to sign on at the Unemployment Benefit Office. In addition, there are many thousands of people at present seeking work who for various reasons cannot claim benefit. Both these groups are now excluded from the figures. In the *National Institute Economic Review* of August 1984, David Metcalf reviewed the quoted unemployment figure for May 1984 – 3.085 million – and made a statistical comparison with the old method of measurement. He calculated that under the old system the figure would have been 3.459 million – a difference of 374,000.[1]

Seasonal adjustment

In order to place the figures into a meaningful context, the statisticians use what is called 'seasonal adjustment'. This is a key figure, because at different times of the year unemployment can be expected to rise and fall naturally. For example, more building workers are employed during the summer than during the winter. Employment in the tourist industries begins to pick up in the spring. Temporary employment is provided in the Christmas period by the Post Office and by large stores. And so on.

What the seasonal adjustment figure tells us is whether an increase or decrease in the employment figures is greater or less than might have been normally expected at that time of year; and thereby it gives us a more accurate comparison to indicate whether the real, underlying trend is up or down.

The significance of the statistics

However the statistics and their manipulations are read, the fact remains that the United Kingdom has a major unemployment problem.

This can be seen by comparing the UK position with the OECD countries. The Organisation for Economic Co-operation and Development is a grouping of the chief industrial nations of Western Europe and North America, together with Japan. It produces comprehensive statistics which are a useful basis for comparison.

The employment situation in Britain is out of step with the rest of the OECD countries. The annual average growth rate of the working-age population is the lowest of all the 24 member countries with the exception of Belgium and Sweden. The number of hours worked per annum per employed person is also lower than most OECD countries.[2]

But the United Kingdom does not merely have a problem in competitiveness. The implications of the figures, for the future of Britain, are very serious. To achieve a level of two million unemployed by 1990 would require a growth rate in employment of 10% over the next five years. The fastest growth rate that the United Kingdom achieved since the last war was between 1959 and 1964, when it was only 6%.

The challenge before us is not only huge. It calls for an achievement that almost doubles anything we have managed since 1945.

The horror, when dealing with such large numbers over a relatively long period of time, is the way in which we get used to the statistics. It is staggering that a level of unemployment of three million plus is now accepted as a fact of life, and something of no particular relevance to those who are employed. Yet the fact remains: the United Kingdom has a peculiarly difficult and complex unemployment problem. It is not going to go away easily.

To a great degree, the future of many of the unemployed lies in the hands of the employed.

One of the most serious myths about unemployment is that the numbers involved are so large that no individual can make a difference. One of the biggest difficulties in persuading people to take action is that when the figures are so big that they do not seem to affect you personally, and the statistics are cold and remote, it is all too easy to have no sense of motivation at all. Yet however we interpret the figures, they represent human suffering on a scale that demands our prayers and our actions.

There is clearly a biblical responsibility here for all of us; to alleviate, and eventually help to bring to an end, a situation in which several million of our fellow human beings are denied the opportunity of work, and so are deprived of two of God's greatest gifts: self-fulfilment and service.

'It's all a matter of getting on your bike'

We have looked a the myth that statistics reflect some sort of absolute indicator of the unemployment situation.

Another common myth is that the unemployed are not trying hard enough to find work, and are not prepared to make sacrifices to do so. The sacrifice that is usually recommended is relocating home and family to a part of the country where work is more readily available.

It is true that one of the most unjust aspects of unemployment is the way in which the pattern of unemployment is so heavily concentrated in certain geographical areas. In this respect there are many similarities with the situation in the 1920s and 1930s.

Northern Ireland, Wales, Scotland and the heavily industrialised north are the worst affected; and the south and southeast, with their emphasis on service industries, light engineering, high technology and major company head offices are least affected. In some of the worst hit areas there are communities currently with 40%–50% levels of unemployment and even higher. In these parts of the country, unemployment is the norm rather than the exception.

Past experience has shown that after a major recession it takes considerable time to re-employ large numbers of people into the paid employment sector. During the 1930s recovery started as early as 1933, yet it was not until 1940, with all the labour demands of the war effort, that unemployment dropped below the one million level.

Also, recovery tends to benefit the south (where unemployment is much lower), more rapidly than the north, or Northern Ireland, where unemployment is high. The financial institutions, service industries, company head offices – all of which are predominantly in the south – are the first to realise the benefits of recovery, before decisions are made to reinvest in the development of the manufacturing, branch office and distribution networks. There is then a further lapse of time before that reinvestment becomes buildings, plant, machinery and vehicles; and it is not until these programmes are complete that jobs will be available in those areas.

Mobility

Unemployed Christians living in the worst-hit areas of unemployment are therefore faced with a dilemma. Since there is little historical warrant for believing that the situation will resolve itself in the short term, what action should they take?

The controversial words of Norman Tebbit – 'Get on your bike and move' – still echo in many people's ears today. The Manpower Services Commission does in fact have grants available for people to attend interviews which are some distance away from their home, and sometimes relocation expenses are paid to people for moving significant distances in order to be nearer their point of work.

But though moving, if you live in a depressed area, may provide a practical solution to the problem of jobs and work, what are the social implications?

Fragmenting structures

In biblical times God prescribed that man should own the land given to him and that the land should be distributed by tribe, by extended family within tribe, and by nuclear family within extended family. The land would become a family inheritance; and therein lay the foundations for a whole community structure, to be continued for generations. The social and moral laws were built round the concepts of community and close family ties. This is evident, for example, in the land allocation prescribed in Numbers 33:54, and is further supported by the various moral codes of the Pentateuch – for example, Leviticus chapters 19–20.

The basis of life in biblical times was therefore that of living and working in a close, interdependent community.

In the Britain of the 1980s, we have witnessed, and are witnessing, the collapse of rural communities, and at the same time the collapse of family interdependence. The result is a huge increase in urban development around the large conurbations, devaluation of family relationships, and increases in social problems – most clearly expressed in the crime statistics and the growing social problem of desperate loneliness.

Towards healthy communities

How would the application of biblical principles alter this situation?

If we were to follow such principles then there is little doubt that our society would have its major emphasis on a developed, strong structure of communities, deriving their economic strength from family businesses where the support and help would come from the family rather than from the banks or consultants; and the mutual trust, ethical business dealings, and just social relationships necessary to maintain such communities would be present.

Were mankind's 'success' to be measured in terms of its progress in human relationships, rather than on its economic standing, it is likely that the United Kingdom would today be regarded in much the same way that the Third World is in the present scheme of things; and that other economically less 'successful' nations would find themselves among the world leaders.

Economists in the United Kingdom frequently identify the immobility of labour as a factor in the unemployment crisis. Recently a scheme has been launched by the Job Centres to create a system of 'town twinning', whereby the needs of an area of high unemployment can be met by the employers of another area. The facts are that the majority of high unemployment areas are in the north, and the areas of high employment are all in the south. The theory, and indeed the practice, includes a programme of training the unemployed to meet needs in skilled labour markets elsewhere.

Our argument is that the funds would be better used to develop the job opportunities of the locality. There are several agencies which have been established for precisely this purpose.

The organisations specialising in this type of initiative are the Council for Small Industries in Rural Areas (CoSIRA), The Welsh Development Agency, the Mid-Wales Development Agency, and the Scottish Development Agency, which are the main agents for the Development Commission.

The primary aims of these agencies are to help develop prosperous communities in rural areas by improving the development of small businesses in the countryside. Help in the form of consultancy, training, providing premises and sometimes finance are the Commission's key services. The regions in which the agencies operate are those which have been designated 'Rural Development Areas', where the needs are greatest. Special emphasis is given to the businesses that will provide additional employment, yet currently employ no more than twenty skilled people. Over 12,800 firms are currently being helped by the Commission, representing more than 77,000 people.[3]

In its literature this organisation makes the significant observation that 'healthy rural communities have an effect on the quality of national life out of proportion to their number.'

If one subscribes to the argument that a lack of job opportunities in a local area ought logically to result in people – particularly the young – moving elsewhere in search of employment, then those who are left behind, often through no fault of their own, will have difficulty in justifying the continued provision of local services in what is left of their community. Schools and hospitals will become subject to closure. Public transport will be reduced. And so begins the spiral of decline.

Sometimes the original community is partially revived by an influx of commuters, but the inevitable side effect of that is an inflation of house prices to a point when the local people can no longer afford to purchase; so many young people who might have found work locally have no option but to move, because that is the only way they will be able to afford a home.

It is a pattern which has, for example, repeated itself tragically in numerous English villages and small towns, which have often become retirement havens or commuter villages after young local families and single people have been forced to relocate to the nearest large city – where often their chances of finding work are not dramatically better than they were at home.

A live community is one that sustains its own health, education, employment and infrastructures, where the biblical principles of social care and social sharing can be practised.

Getting 'on your bike' will often mean leaving that community, and its needs, behind.

Technological unemployment

Another common myth is that unemployment is high because new industrial technologies are destroying jobs. In fact one of the most widely-argued debates in the overall discussion of unemployment at present concerns the extent of the impact of technology on employment.

The case against technology

Some argue a case along the following lines: We are going through a technological revolution. On the shop floor and in many other areas of work, technology is gradually replacing human labour. Eventually machines will be the national workforce.

This revolution, it is argued, is one of the root causes of our present unemployment problems. There should therefore be a concentration of effort upon leisure industries, and encouraging the unemployed to use their time in a socially and personally constructive way. Otherwise, enforced boredom will produce antisocial behaviour and disrupt the rest of society. This argument is of course a variant on the 'Satan finds some mischief yet/For idle hands to do' argument.

This argument has a good deal of common sense on its side.

There is no doubt that technology has had its impact on the job market, and that it has done so ever since the Industrial Revolution. It is also true that automation can produce cost benefits to an employer, though this too has been the case for many years. Ever since the Industrial Revolution, when steam looms and threshing machines were introduced, automation has played a part in the employment debate.

Technology and rising demand

However, if technology is seen as an ogre then one of two assumptions is being made. One is that human demand is a fixed quantity, and that the increasing proportion of it supplied by technology must mean that the proportion left to manual labour diminishes accordingly. The other is that output to meet that demand is limited by the capital available, and that machinery consumes so much capital that even were it fully used no company could afford enough machinery to employ its entire workforce.

In both cases the argument points to the need to reduce levels of technology. In both cases the argument is wrong.

The evidence[4] is that since the commencement of high unemployment figures in 1974, and with the exception of the years 1979 and 1984, we have not fully utilised our production capacity, and that our utilisation of resources has in fact declined below the historic average. When high unemployment began, productivity actually fell. During 1984, industry recorded unusually high increases in productivity, but these were not matched by comparable meteoric rises in unemployment – which is what might have been expected if the 'technology-ogre' argument were valid.

There is simply not enough evidence to prove the correlation between demand/productivity and enforced unemployment, when viewed in the light of the macro-economic situation. There is evidence that automation has *saved* jobs in the United Kingdom from an onslaught of labour-cheap products from the Third World, and that technology in this situation has been a major contributor to the security of jobs.

In fact in the traditional homelands of high technology –

Germany, Japan and the United States – the effect has been to lower prices and consequently lift demand. As a result, employment has increased.

A similar situation exists in British Leyland UK, where there has been massive mechanisation. The company is presently recruiting additional labour.

But it is in the United States that the greatest advantages of technology have been experienced; not only in the new industries of development, production and installation, but also in the huge growth of associated service industries such as computers and data processing.

There is a good argument that one of the causes of unemployment in Britain is that the country has already delayed too long in investing in new technologies. Both because of an unwillingness to take risks and because of the difficult financial climate, capital reinvestment programmes, particularly in industry, have been lethargic. The results are:

1. The technologies are bought in from abroad;

2. British products are less competitive; and

3. The door is left wider open for importers of such products from either the labour-cheap countries or those that have applied the new technologies and therefore have more sophisticated manufacturing facilities.

In the end, automation is as much about job retention as it is about job creation.

There are many examples that demonstrate how technologies that are primarily developed for major capital programmes do have major new consumer applications which develop as a by-product. One of the most obvious examples is the home computer industry. This industry alone has generated thousands of new jobs, not only in the assembly of the equipment but also in the development of software, distribution – advertising, retailing and so on – and all this in an industry which did not exist ten years ago.

The wider benefits of technology

There are many examples of the way in which technology has made great strides in eliminating aspects of work which are dehumanising. Hundreds of tasks which made no creative demands on those who performed them, or which involved sheer mechanical repetition, are now performed by machines.

In a recent survey conducted by Northcott and Rogers under the heading of 'General employment implications' the authors state that unemployment affects the application of microelectronics in manufacturing industries. Those affected

> between 1981 and 1983 appear to have amounted to an average of only about 1 person per year per establishment and about 17,000 people per year in total . . . Moreover, much of the increase has taken the form of natural wastage, with the result that the actual redundancies appear to have been running at the rate of only about 6,000 a year, only half of them involuntary, an even smaller figure in national terms.[5]

History would tend to indicate that once the new technologies have been accommodated, all sectors of society will benefit. For example, societies that lived through the second Industrial Revolution in the nineteenth century are much better off economically than those that benefited from the first Industrial Revolution a century earlier. On the other hand, in both cases the major technological innovations were condemned by many at the time as a socio-economic disaster.

All this is not to say that technology does not have any effect on the unemployment problem, but rather that it is not – in the macro-economic sense – a *major* cause.

The needs of the individual

There are obviously people who get caught in the 'ability trap' and have a real difficulty in contemplating retraining. They need specialist help in reviewing what skills they have, and the direction which their career should take.

In the same way the educational system ought to be looking forward to the needs of the 1990s, and planning ways to equip our young people with the adaptability that will be essential in dealing with a society of rapid change.

That is perhaps the essence of the problem. The day when it was the reasonable ambition of a person to have a career for life is now largely over. The career pattern of the future holds the possibility that a single working life will involve perhaps five or six changes of direction. Being prepared to retrain and adapt to this changing work pattern is critical, and not only for those presently in work. We need to place great emphasis on the need for retraining facilities for the unemployed.

This issue is dealt with in greater detail on p. 91, under the heading of Training Workshops.

The leisure industry solution

Many people, in accordance with some economists and forecasters, believe that there are just too many factors militating against the unemployed. High unemployment, they argue, is now a fact of social life, and we had better start planning programmes to occupy the time of the unemployed with alternative pursuits.

The answer, it is often suggested, lies in the development of the leisure industry. Leisure activities – by which are meant recreation, entertainment, and hobbies – could well form part of a strategy to deal with the increased time that people who have no jobs will have.

But how does the unemployed person pay for such facilities? Should we be lobbying for free television, video, sports centres, ten-pin bowling alleys, dance centres, Bingo and the like – all specifically for the jobless?

A basic misunderstanding lies at the heart of the argument. The misunderstanding is only partly to do with the fact that it is patronising in the extreme to assume that because somebody has no job, he or she will automatically turn into a mindless zombie who has to be somehow entertained.

What is forgotten is that leisure hours should be a

complement to working hours – not a substitute for them. Leisure hours are fun, indeed, because they are so scarce; there is a clear difference between flopping down in front of a television, exhausted from a day's work, and simply watching television all day for want of anything more interesting to occupy the time.

In our opinion what really demoralises and dehumanises is not solely the lack of paid employment, but the lack of *work*.

In Genesis 1:26 we find that man's dominion over nature rests in our likeness to God. Our potential for creative work is an essential part of our God-like humanness. Destroy that, and an important element of our humanity is destroyed with it.

It is largely through work of various kinds that service to God and man is performed. By definition, only through work is life's satisfaction to be obtained. The God who is revealed to us in Genesis as a creator is also revealed to us as one who having created all things pronounced them 'good'. As such, he enjoys perfect job satisfaction!

All people – whether employed, semi-employed, under-employed, unemployed or retired – need an environment in which they can work creatively. An outlet for our natural creative energies is therefore essential. It is through this activity that we can receive the blessings of service, a sense of purpose and an element of job satisfaction. It *may* come through the work we do as paid employment – but it *need* not do so. It does not demean somebody to earn a living sweeping roads, and it is not essential that that job should in some way satisfy his desire for creative work – provided it can be satisfied in other ways.

The Fourth Commandment, it is often forgotten, is not just a command to rest for one day. It is also a command to work for six! The emphasis is not on payment, but on work. For many of the employed this means working in the home on the sixth day, or working at a hobby, or gardening.

So if there is no paid employment at all, the individual is not deprived of the opportunity to live a fulfilled, creative life. Other channels exist – and must be found – through which that God-given creativity can be expressed.

Working at finding a new job, working at getting a new

business into shape, working on a community project, decorating the homes of the elderly, gardening, pursuing a creative hobby – all these encompass the use of creative occupation in a way that most leisure pursuits cannot.

Free bowling alleys for the unemployed would offer only limited scope for this creative fulfilment. There are many other occupations that offer much more. This is not a middle-class, pious or right-wing approach to the problem, but one that is founded on the biblical fact that men and women are creative. Christians must pioneer ways to provide facilities by which skills can be learned and practised and inborn gifts can be discovered.

Often it is the continued waste of time, by mindless preoccupations enjoyed at undisciplined hours of the day, that can develop the bad habits that create the psychological problems and make re-entry into the job market so difficult. The church must be preaching the need to find answers, but at the same time it must take direct, considered action, in order to give society at large and politicians alike an example to follow, not merely rhetoric. For example, for many years now, congregations in churches throughout the country who have inherited older buildings have realised that those buildings are too large, inefficient in space, expensive to heat and maintain. We should be looking to the potential that they possess. They could provide work as modernisation projects, or could be adapted to become resource centres for new training courses (an example of this attitude put into practice in a church situation is given on p. 125).

Using one's time in creative service in a structured fashion not only better prepares one for the demands of paid employment, but it also makes one a better candidate for employment. Above all, it enables one to find an element of fulfilment as a human being, to bring some benefit to the community and to glorify the Creator.

Long-term unemployment

The precise extent to which the unemployment statistics really do reflect the real situation in human terms is a mystery to many people, and is surrounded by many misconceptions.

One misconception – which is understandable – is that the unemployed are a continuously changing group of people, from which everybody sooner or later escapes; and another, equally understandable, is that the unemployed comprise a group of people from which nobody escapes and to which many new members are continuously added.

But neither is true. The fact is that thousands of people do get work every month and no longer figure in the statistics. The statistics, in fact, contribute to the misunderstanding because of the method of compilation. They merely represent a sample taken at a single moment. If the number of people finding work at that moment is lower than the number of those losing their jobs and receiving unemployment or Social Security benefit, then the unemployment figure is said to have risen.

So if the assumption were to be made that everybody does eventually get work, the unemployment figure would merely represent the increase in the time it is currently taking to find a job.

But the truth is that the statistics mean much more than that. They reflect every mix of human circumstances and types; between jobs, out of work, short-term unemployed; labourer, managing director, family man, single girl – all of whom have to come to terms with their own particular situation. Having confronted the sheer horror of the overall numbers, one should attempt to look, in depth, at what the statistics are really telling us.

As we have described elsewhere in this book, the most debilitating thing about unemployment is how, in a short space of time, the unemployed person can move from hope through despair to total aimlessness.

I want to suggest that even more important than the overall statistics of unemployment are the figures relating to long-term joblessness.

To isolate these figures and give them meaning, I propose to examine the subject in two sections; long-term youth unemployment, and long-term adult unemployment.

Long-term youth unemployment

Without doubt, this is the most dramatic sector of the long-term unemployed community. There was a time when high youth unemployment was thought to be something to do with under 18-year-olds undergoing a brief spell of joblessness. Today, with the problem having been prevalent since 1979 and now affecting college and university leavers as well as school leavers, all under 25-year-olds run a high risk of unemployment.

The facts are simple and unambiguous.

One in two under 18-year-olds cannot get work.

One in every five under 25-year-olds is out of work. 1,286,183 under 25-year-olds were claiming the dole in January 1985.

Teenagers (that is, 16- to 19-year-olds) are twice as likely as adults to be signing on.

Long-term unemployment for the under-25 age group grew by one third in 1983 compared with 1982, and was 57% worse than in 1979.

The grim statistics

Bearing in mind that the method of calculating the totals of the unemployed was changed in October 1982, it is estimated that the change from counting only unemployed benefit claimants rather than people registered for work removed over 100,000 under 25-year-olds from the statistics. About 55,000 of them had been unemployed for over a year.

If, therefore, we were to compare like with like, we would probably find that nearly 1.4 million young people were out of work in 1983. If we then add to those the youngsters involved in the MSC programmes, the total of under 25-year-olds without real gainful employment, is approximately 1.7 million. This figure compares with a total of 1.4 million *of all ages* only four years previously.

The figures I have quoted – all freely available from the *Department of Employment Gazette*[6] – are, or course, compiled on a national basis. But as with the overall figures, there are regions of the country which have a much worse situation; for example, in the West Midlands 37% of the under-25 age group have been out of work for over a year, and 15% have been out of work for over two years.

In April 1985 there were 74,623 young people in Britain, between the ages of 20 and 24, who had not worked for more than three years.

22,035 19-year-olds had not worked for more than two years.

23,012 18-year-olds had not worked for more than eighteen months.

7,606 17-year-olds had not worked for more than 15 months.[7]

The figures add up to 127,276 of the nation's young people who may never have worked. They are the long term youth unemployed and will have appalling difficulty in finding a job.

Under which biblical law can such huge numbers of our young people be denied the self-respect of earning a wage, or indeed the opportunity for creative outlets?

Rites of passage

Overall, as at April 1985, around 359,042 people under 25 years old have been unemployed for over 12 months.[8]

To put these figures into context, it must be said that from 1978 to 1983, job opportunities for 16-year-old school-leavers fell by 56%. The number of apprenticeships fell by over 70%.

All societies mark the transition from childhood and adolescence to adulthood by some ritual observance. There is no doubt that our society is structured in such a way that that transition is marked by obtaining work. Its impact is heavily coloured by the impact of earning a wage. The move from total financial dependence to relative independence is confirmed in the sense of pride with which a youngster parades his first pay packet, like a hard-won trophy; it symbolises the arrival in the ranks of adulthood.

By contrast, unemployment is a state of adolescent near-limbo. The unemployed youngster is no longer a student within the educational community, but is not yet an adult living within the community of those working. The no-man's-land of unemployment has no real community context, nor any accepted social role. It is rejection.

That period in a young person's life should be a period of exciting change, of new things to learn and new people to meet. For hundreds of thousands, it is a time of rejection and failure, frequently leading to severe depression.

It is upon this age group, their abilities, talents, motivation to work and general outlook on the world, that the country will depend in the next few decades.

Or will it?

Most employers prefer, when making their hiring decisions, to employ those who have been out of work for the shortest time, or have never been out of work at all. Perhaps we will have a gap in our employment structure similar to that which occurred following the Second World War when so many of our young people died. We could become known as the society which created a generation of the walking dead.

Today's young people remain jobless while the habits and aspirations of parents and schoolteachers are still ringing in their ears. They have the costume, they have learned their lines, they have even obtained the part; but for some reason inexplicable to them, the play has been abandoned.

How do we really believe the psychological needs of these youngsters are going to be fulfilled? By satisfying their material needs and taking out their frustrations on themselves, their families and the rest of society? Or by abandoning their material needs and existing on meagre allowances, not going out of doors, receding into their own shells in a state of manic depression? Or a combination of both?

The dominant adjustment to unemployment in the thirties was demonstration, followed by violence, followed by despair and giving up. Already in Britain manifestations of all three stages have been seen. Perhaps the most worrying of all is the growing number of youngsters who are now apathetic and discouraged and no longer search for jobs. They have adjusted to a welfare-supported existence, and have given up not only the search, but sometimes also the willingness to enter employment.

It is in this context that we must try to teach self-worth and the perspective of how God values man and determines his worth. It is an enormous task.

It is so easy to adopt stereotyped attitudes. Because the number of those unemployed is so large, almost everybody knows of somebody who is jobless. One often overhears conversations.

> 'I don't think he/she even *wants* a job now.'
> 'He/she just doesn't seem to want to try any more.'
> 'Sometimes he/she doesn't get up until 11 a.m.'

How often such comments are made in a critical, condemnatory way, as if the major blame should rest on the unemployed person, without any regard for what he or she has been through.

It cannot be emphasised enough that the young people of this country are currently bearing a massive burden. Their lives are being seriously scarred by our inability, failure and lack of enterprise in finding them work.

Long-term adult unemployment

If the definition of 'long-term unemployment' is taken to be 'unemployed for more than one year', the total number of long-term unemployed in the United Kingdom is (in April 1985) 1,334,161.[9]

Young people under 25 represent, as we have seen, the largest sector. However, after allowing for them, there are, according to the published statistics, some 975,119 adults who have been unemployed for longer than twelve months.

It is a tragic irony that the worst sector of the long-term unemployed adults is made up of those who were born during, or before, the only time in our history when unemployment was comparable to what it is today. They are those aged 55 and over.

Since the change in the method of counting the unemployed affected those over the age of sixty, the official figures do not cover all adults to retirement age. However, 178,147 adults aged between 55 and 59 have currently been unemployed for more than a year. From January 1979 to January 1985, the overall growth in unemployment in that age group has been 181.3%.

In exactly the same way that young people have been brought up with expectations only to find them frustrated by the current employment situation, so the person who has worked for most of his life has come to expect his life to follow a predictable course.

For the 55-year-old or older, history has taught him that certain things can reasonably be depended on. For some there is the expectation of many more years of earning a living. For most, there is the expectation of working through until the age of 65 and saving up for a secure retirement. (The numbers of those making special financial arrangements for early retirement are often widely publicised, but such people are in a minority.)

Elsewhere in this book the concept of early retirement is discussed, applauded and encouraged – in the context of an overall plan, financial recompense for those involved, and a programme for helping to occupy those who have retired early with creative pursuits. The prime emphasis, moreover, is on the 60-plus age group.

But the figures we are quoting here are for the 55- to 59-year-olds, whose abrupt loss of employment certainly was not planned in the majority of cases, who have not received adequate financial recompense, and for whom no organised alternatives to work exist. It takes considerable understanding to appreciate the frustration of being capable of work, having years of experience to offer, with no desire at all to sit at home; to watch one's savings, which had been put aside to provide comfort in retirement, dwindling as they are dipped into again and again until, at the age of 65, full retirement pay is made available.

It is effectively the horrors of the thirties repeating themselves.

Though I have emphasised the under 25-year-olds and the over 55-year-olds, the plight of those in between must not be minimised. To be out of work during the period of life in which one should be at the height of one's powers to earn, and in which the demands of raising and supporting a family are greatest, is nothing short of tragic.

The counselling needs of the unemployed are discussed in another part of this book. (See p. 102.) What I have done here is to demonstrate the very worst aspects of the problem in the stark reality of the statistics, and to suggest their true implications.

But such an exercise is useless if it merely adds to our intellectual knowledge of the present economic and social crisis. The unemployment debate has too many experts and too few activists.

What difference ought knowing the numbers make?

Those of us who are in Christian families – especially those of us who are parents of young children – and those who teach or guide the young should ask ourselves: what expectations are we imposing upon our own children? How are we and our schools preparing our young people for the time when they leave school, college or university? Have we discussed, as a family, what would happen if those in the family at present in work were to lose their jobs? How would we cope with it and adjust to the new situation? Could we, as families, adapt to a situation where one member – perhaps the breadwinner – was out of work for a year or more? What sort of help and support would we be able to give?

Such discussions are much better before the event than after. And the event, sadly, is not going to become less common. Even an unexpected upturn in the economy is not likely to provide solutions immediately. An unpublished MSC report produced in 1982 points out:

> It seems unlikely that the problem will be solved quickly by the working of the market . . . The evidence of the last 20 years suggests that long-term unemployed people would be the last to benefit in terms of finding new jobs.[10]

So the questions need prayerful consideration. It is all too easy, as with reports of appalling accidents, to put our heads in the sand and retreat into the illusion of 'it couldn't happen here'.

It often demands courage to face the most unpleasant issues of life, and even more courage to share these concerns with others. Yet we are taught that in doing so we receive strength.

Our society is not merely changing. It has changed.

The Bible presents answers to contemporary practical problems just as much as it does to spiritual issues. It is now that the Church as a body of Christians must take the lead, both corporately and individually. We must ensure that there is a comprehensive understanding of the difficulties facing so many in our society, and we must be prepared to work towards creating action programmes that will alleviate the mental anguish that this particular issue is causing to both the younger and older generations.

In the past, the Church and its members fought hard and faithfully against enormous social abuses; one might think of Wesley and Wilberforce, to take but two examples. Today the call is the same. We cannot be content to allow such huge numbers of our society to be simply written off. We know too well the contribution they have to make, and their true value in the sight of God, to rest easy when they are dehumanised and dispirited through a situation not of their own making.

Female employment and unemployment

One misconception that many have about unemployment is that women are taking jobs that, if left for the male breadwinner, would contribute to solving the problem.

This is not always a sexist argument; it is sometimes argued as a genuine cause of the unemployment crisis. But though female employment is a relatively recent significant factor in the overall employment picture, abolishing it is not the easy solution that it is sometimes thought to be.

It was hardly realised at the time, but the magnificent response that British women made to the Second World War effort, by working in factories, offices, hospitals and distribution industries, was to establish a change in work patterns that was set to continue on into the future.

Statistics[11] reveal that by mid-1983, female labour represented 40.4% of the total work force and 41.5% of all people employed in the civilian labour force.

The fact that women seem to be less affected by the unemployment crisis than are men is often cited as a criticism, the implication being that too high a proportion of the available jobs are being held by women. However, the criticism should be placed into context. In 1983, for example, 400,000 women were non-claimant unemployed people, whereas there were only 200,000 men registered as non-claimant unemployed. Also, of the 9.5 million women employed in the civilian labour force, four million were part-time employees, whilst of the 11 million men employed in the civilian labour force, only 700,000 are recorded as part-time employees.

At the same time that this shift in availability of female labour has been taking place, the job market has also been shifting. Between 1971 and 1981, the male-dominated industries such as construction, mining, transport, production and agriculture have seen major declines in labour usage, whilst those in which female labour has commanded a more significant role (such as education, welfare, health and other services) show substantial percentage increases. So the figures are misleading.

It has sometimes been suggested that one possible way of contributing to a solution to the unemployment problem would be to reverse the social trend that has brought so many women into paid employment. That is, in particular, to encourage married women to go back to looking after the home. Yet the emancipatory struggle ought to continue, and it will. Despite the Sex Discrimination Acts, the work that women obtain is often hard won, involving less pay and frequently fewer promotion prospects. In 1983, the average gross weekly earnings of male full-time manual employees was £140.10. For female workers it was £87.90. For non-manual workers the weekly averages were males, £190.70; females, £115.10.[12]

The suggestion that female activity in the economy should be reduced must be strongly resisted on both theological and social grounds.

It is clear that women play a vital and a critical role in the total employment picture, and they make a considerable contribution to the nation's wealth. Also, women have the same need for creative expression as men, and many will have experienced a sense of isolation, of lack of personal and social status, despite the fact that they are fully involved in household work.

There is a real need to challenge the old evangelical ideology of domesticity that only serves to restrict personal choice, rather than opening up the freedom of life's opportunites in the creative dimension of our society.

Even single women are victims of the same prejudices and inhibitions. They deserve to be treated with total equality in the labour market.

As far as work relates to marriages, in 1983 wives worked in 58% of marriages, and in 4% of marriages the wife is the sole member of the partnership who is in work.

In 1981 there were 240,000 families which were earning below the supplementary benefit level, and some 1,130,000 families involving 3,840,000 people were earning less than 140% of the supplementary benefit level. Obviously many of these families depend on the wife's earnings for survival. Also, despite the fact that support for child-minding is almost non-existent, 42% of single-parent mothers manage to gain employment to support their children.

So female employment makes a major financial contribution to those families in particularly deprived circumstances. It is clearly untrue to believe that women take jobs at the expense of men; they have their rightful contribution to make to the national economy.

Obviously, the idea of work as a continuous, lifelong occupation is not so prevalent among women as men for obvious reasons. But this in no way devalues the need, the right, or the contribution. It is now commonplace for women to expect to work full time until the birth of their first child.

Most women expect to return to the job market at some time following the birth of their children. In fact legislation exists virtually throughout Europe, whereby employers are obliged to re-hire women who want to return to work within a given period after pregnancy.

However, in this aspect of female employment I believe that the law can, while protecting the job, also create some extreme pressures on the mother. Before the legislation, between 1950 and 1954, the average time-lapse between the birth of the last child in the family and the mother returning to work was seven and a half years, whereas between 1975 and 1979, the time-lapse had reduced to three and a half years. There is increasing evidence to show that more and more women are re-entering the job market between the births of their children. Bearing in mind that these figures are averages, many women are returning to work before their children are even old enough to attend playgroup. Though one has to allow for the economic and psychological pressures that may well exist for a woman to re-enter the job market as soon as possible, the responsibilities of the Christian parent to the child's upbringing must take precedence.

Between 1981 and 1983, 25% of married mothers with children under the age of five were working. But of those with the greatest financial pressures – single mothers with children under five – only 18% were working. This may be related to the level of family support available, or to a difference in attitude, between single and married mothers, to their children.

As we have seen, the Bible makes clear that there is a need for creative expression in humanity. Also the family must be financially taken care of. But the Bible also places a fundamental emphasis on the responsibilities of parenthood.

Biblically, the responsibility of parents is to express concern, love and compassion for their children and to hold the personal responsibilities of bringing them up in the truth. The privilege of receiving such a gift from God as the creation of a whole being, is something to be taken with the utmost seriousness.

I believe, therefore, that these commands should overrule

all other considerations. To emphasise the need to work over and above all biblical responsibilities of parenthood is wrong.

In situations therefore where the mother has the most marketable skills and both are unemployed, the father should consider supporting the family by reversing the roles and doing all that is possible to support the wife in her capacity as breadwinner and mother.

The challenge to the Church, and to all Christians, is to recognise the tremendous contribution female employment makes, while at the same time acknowledging the problems it incurs.

What we need is for Christians to ensure that equal opportunities, both *for* employment and *in* employment, become a reality. Major efforts are needed to organise part-time jobs that can integrate with playgroup times, school times and school holidays. In this way, the desire and the need to work can be accommodated to the biblical demands of motherhood.

The particular demands the Bible makes concerning fatherless children, and God's clear, special concern for them, give every Christian the burden especially to help the single-parent mother in her plight of trying to raise her children while possibly having the extra burden of being unemployed.

Perhaps the cost of playgroups is beyond her pocket. The free supply of such a service may serve to enhance the child's interpersonal and play skills; it may also afford the opportunity of a part-time job in which the mother can have the opportunity not only of expression outside the ties of her family, but also providing for her children.

So, far from encouraging the reduction of female employment, I am arguing for Christians to enhance the justice, opportunity and care for promoting female employment within the framework of what the Bible teaches.

Conclusion

We have considered some of the major myths and misconceptions that are prevalent today regarding unemployment.

Clearly, the correction of misunderstanding is an important first step in coming to terms with any major social problem.

But knowledge, even informed knowledge, can create sympathy but can do little to change things. Change demands action.

In the remainder of this book, we will consider a programme of action.

Part 3: Projects for Action

Introduction

Many churches, individual Christians and secular organisations are involved in alleviating the problems of the unemployed, and a great deal of work is being done. This is all valuable and helpful, and a list of these organisations, together with details of their activities, is included in this book.

However, our plan in this book is to emphasise ways in which Christians, acting as individuals and also as members of local churches, can take action, both in their work environment and in their local church neighbourhood. Some are approaches which have been tried successfully in churches in Britain; others are new ideas, based on experience of the employment market and the business world.

To put into practice the suggestions which are contained in the following pages demands commitment, tact and understanding. But it is our belief that these suggestions could dramatically affect the jobless figures which are such a blight on our society.

No scheme will provide all the answers, and certainly even were all our suggestions taken up by large numbers of people, the unemployment problems would still be a problem. If it were that easy to prescribe solutions, it would have been solved years ago.

Nevertheless, the projects that we suggest do have both a biblical and an economic foundation. If they were seriously put into practice they could make a major dent in the problem without creating more overmanning or provoking rampant inflation.

It does nothing for the unemployed simply to blame governments for not carrying out one line of economic policy or another. Indeed, that attitude – that solutions can be created only at government level – can lead to the belief that any individual action at a personal level is useless. From that, inactivity naturally results.

But just as we are called to Jesus Christ as individuals, so also our responsibility to carry out his commandments is an individual responsibility. Nobody else can become a Christian on our behalf, and nobody else can remain a Christian on our behalf.

Jesus calls us to be activists. He requires us not merely to allow his teachings to touch the surface of our lives, but to allow him to enter into every part of what we do, how we think and, indeed, who we are.

And this includes the time we spend at work just as much as the time we spend at church. Those of us who are in work have a privilege and an asset which many in our society do not have. We therefore need to think seriously about what the Bible says is expected of those who have much.

Biblical giving

One of the central themes of Christian discipleship is that of giving. The Bible does not teach giving as a legal duty, nor does it restrict the whole matter to purely financial terms. Biblical giving – more properly, sharing – is a natural outflowing of the Christian's gratitude to God and love for his fellow human beings.

When we consider the unemployment issue, it is impossible to separate it from the biblical concept of giving.

The scriptural emphasis is on compassion in the presence of God and on giving for the right motive; it should be done in God's name. Frequently giving is related to righteousness; not because it justifies a man (Paul emphatically discounts that idea in Romans 3–4), but simply because it is right to give and because God gives us the resources out of which we can give. Paul does not teach that Christians should work merely because it is preferable to immoral ways of providing for one's needs, but because work provides that resource from which we are able to give to others less fortunate:

> He who has been stealing must steal no longer, but must work, doing something useful with his own hands, that he may have something to share with those in need (Eph 4:28).

In Matthew 6:1–4 we are also commanded by Jesus not to give ostentatiously. His emphasis is on the fact that giving is a blessing to the giver as well as to the receiver.

If the Bible talked of giving solely in terms of money, then the only Christians eligible to experience this particular blessing from God would be those who had disposable income over and above their own essential needs. But this is not the biblical teaching, as is obvious from the experience of the Early Church: 'All the believers were one in heart and mind. No one claimed that any of his possessions was his own, but they shared everything they had.' (Acts 4:32) If that is so, then clearly giving a job is no different to giving a loaf of bread, a sum of money or anything else; it is just as much a blessing and is just as much subject to biblical discipline.

Work agencies

But how, in practice, can an individual give somebody else a job? If we look round the average church we will find few members of the congregation who are employers, and many churches have nobody in that situation.

The answer is that while few individuals can offer somebody a full week's paid employment, a number of individuals, pooling their work resources effectively and with a certain amount of co-ordinating management, can.

There are jobs that we all do in the home that could be done equally well, and in some cases – where our own skills are limited – much better, by somebody who is unemployed. It needs to be emphasised that no one person is likely to have enough work of this nature to employ one person full time, and for that matter most small groups would not have enough either. But if a church were to take on a project along these lines and its members see the venture as a corporate responsibility, the results could be truly rewarding.

The proposal we are putting forward is that a church that has such a vision should consider forming a 'work agency'. Like a housing agency or a theatrical agency, the function of this agency would be to bring together those who wished to buy and those who possessed the resources to meet their needs. Unlike the employment agency or the job agency, which both exist mainly to service the *job* market, the purpose of the work agency would be literally to sell *work*, often in quite small units, and to act as co-ordinating organisation so that those whose work was being sold would end up with reasonably continuous employment.

It would operate in the following way. The unemployed of the area would register with the agency, which would interview them and maintain a register of skills, domestic background (availability for evening work, etc.), references, flexibility, mobility, and any other details which would contribute to an accurate employment profile for each person.

The church members who are supporting the scheme should then commit at least one job each fortnight to the agency. These jobs would range from relatively unskilled work (such as mowing the lawn, cleaning the car, digging the garden or other domestic chores), to more skilled work (such as painting and decorating or small building jobs). The essential factors should be:

1. The work given should be entirely new, in the sense that it does not deprive an existing worker of work that he or she would have done had not the scheme been in operation. It should be work that the sponsoring individuals would normally have done themselves.

2. The market rate for the work should be paid, plus sufficient to cover the overhead expenses including travel to the agency.

3. The employee should report for work at the agency, be given the schedule of jobs for the day, and be paid for the week's work following that in which he worked.

4. All statutory deductions should be made by the agency.

An essential clause in the terms of employment should be that payment is dependent upon the work being completed and reasonably conducted.

There is a balance to be maintained between the fact that the sponsoring individuals are actually *giving* in a real sense (in that the alternative is to do what they would have done otherwise – carry out the work themselves with no financial outlay), and the fact that if the unemployed person is to be helped in any real sense the agency must be run to the same standards of competence and professionalism as would be called for in a work situation being run for profit and competitiveness.

The basis of the scheme is to use the fruits of those in work to share with, and give legitimate work to, the unemployed. The way in which such a scheme is constructed is designed to re-introduce the unemployed person to the disciplines of a regular job, to maintain proper working hours, and to pay the person who has done the work in a way that preserves the dignity that genuine work, well done, should provide (which is why payment must be made direct to the agency, never to the person who has just completed the work).

It takes quite a large number of people to sponsor a work agency effectively. It may well be that your church could not by itself sustain such a project. However, that should not be a deterrent, but rather a stimulus to discuss the idea with other local churches, to provide a united act of practical help in line with biblical principles. It could be the beginning of an exciting time of local co-operation and fellowship between neighbouring churches!

Facts and figures

Assuming that the average job would take approximately two hours, and that (allowing for breaks and travel) the average working day would be six working hours, it would need approximately 30 people, employing someone once a fortnight for two hours, to give that one person full employment. Similarly, assuming that the agency would need to charge approximately £4 per hour in order to cover all the costs we have so far mentioned, the 'cost of giving' for the sponsoring individual would be no more than £4 per week (for which, of course, he or she would receive labour in return). On these figures, 120 sponsoring individuals could provide continuous work for four people.

The person responsible for organising the agency would need to maintain good communication with the sponsoring members so that they are constantly informed of the skills available, and are therefore in a good position to assess what work would be best placed with the agency.

Typical figures for an agency might be similar to the following (I give two figures in each case, to show that workable figures can be calculated to suit any prevailing local rates of pay for comparable work):

Pay	£ 2.50 per hour	(£ 1.50)
Employer's National Insurance	£ 0.28 per hour	(£ 0.16)
Hourly total	**£ 2.78 per hour**	**(£ 1.66)**
Gross weekly pay (30 working hours)	£ 75.00 per week	(£45.00)
Employer's National Insurance	£ 8.40 per week	(£ 4.80)
Total salary cost per employee ...	**£ 83.40 per week**	**(£49.80)**
Income: say £4 (£2.50) per hour on 30 working hours	£120.00 per week	(£75.00)
Less salary cost per employee	£ 83.40 per week	(£49.80)
Balance to set against defraying overheads and travel	**£ 36.60 per week** **per person.**	**(£25.20)**

The balance would be sufficient to cover the cost of stationery, telephone, travel, insurance, and even the rent and rates, heating, light and power of a small office – though working from a home would reduce the costs.

Indeed, if the project could sustain four full-time workers, then it becomes clear from the figures given above that £146.40 (£100.80) would be available for overheads and may well support an unemployed person to be in charge of the agency – thus creating a fifth job. The scheme would require somebody who was capable of communicating effectively both with the unemployed people and the participating sponsors. Ability to handle simple accounts would also be necessary, and of course the person in charge would also be dealing with PAYE and invoicing.

It should be added that the figures would vary from area to area depending on the state of the labour market. But in a high percentage of situations it would generate more income for the unemployed person joining the scheme than that person would receive on unemployment pay or supplementary benefit. It would also be part of the scheme that employees should be allowed time to attend interviews as and when necessary.

It may well be the case that such a scheme is best used in conjunction with the local Job Centre, where the opportunities it offers can be extended to the non-Christian unemployed. In fact, the Job Centres themselves do offer a temporary job scheme.

Each implementation of the 'work agency' concept would be unique in some way, closely reflecting the particular job situation in its locality. But the principle would remain the same; that is, job creation, achieved by those who are employed sharing the benefits of employment with those who are unemployed.

Pay cuts for jobs

The Chancellor and many eminent economists have frequently suggested that one reason why unemployment remains at such a high level is because the labour costs in Britain are still far too high.

Some argue that this is because of the free market-place in the United Kingdom, and reflects a failure of economic policy – and that remedying that failure would solve the problem; others argue that an overall reduction of relative labour costs can be achieved by the mass employment of young people at the low end of the earning scale. Another argument is that the labour market is still not sufficiently free of union controls, and that the greater market freedom that would exist if it were to be liberated from those controls would mean that wages would be lower. The essential argument is that if it cost less to employ people then employers would be encouraged to increase their workforces.

The intention of this section is not to get involved in the economic debate, but to comment upon the basic premise. It is certainly true; but it is only true selectively.

Where companies are under pressure from their shareholders to achieve growth in profits, it is certain that lower wages would not automatically lead to higher levels of employment, but would lead to lower pay overheads; these would reflect higher profits and therefore higher dividends to the shareholders.

But what if the company is budgeting for *real* growth, as opposed to profit growth? Under such circumstances a voluntary wage reduction, or voluntary pay freeze would enable the employer to increase jobs in direct proportion to productivity – in other words, as expressed by the ratio of unit cost divided by the number of units produced. Far more jobs would be created than would otherwise be the case.

Similarly, in a labour-intensive and highly competitive market, a wage reduction would be reflected in low unit costs, which may allow a lower selling price. This would increase the volume of sales because of the increased market share achieved by the price reduction; and that would mean more jobs. The argument particularly holds good when a company is facing potential bankruptcy because the business is operating beyond its gross profit. It was in the early 1980s that the employees of many major American companies demonstrated their readiness to take wage reductions rather than lose jobs, thus giving the companies time to recover whilst preserving employment.

The Christian at work

If Christian employees are to take the challenge of their faith into the world of their work, then this is certainly an issue that they should raise at union, worker committee and management levels. The fact that this debate is not taking place in businesses throughout the United Kingdom is, sadly, a reflection of man's greed.

How does one get the debate started? Three requirements are absolutely essential.

1. A genuine, serious preparedness on the part of the Christian employee to take a wage reduction – or, at the least, a wage standstill.

2. A preparedness to argue the case for this idea with fellow workers, and thereby obtain support and practical commitment.

3. A discussion with management about the implications were such action to be taken, and the securing of a written agreement as to the absolute monetary effect, and the effect in terms of employment, should such action be taken. What one is after is an undertaking that the workers' commitment should be translated into jobs for others.

It could well happen that the right challenge to the right company at the right time would have the desired effect. So assuming that a group of workers was interested enough in pursuing this concept to secure action at management level, what results could be expected?

It would certainly maximise job growth in the company. With inflation running at – say – 5%, a wage standstill of a year's duration might well produce the same figure in increased jobs. A 5% *decrease*, by the same token, would effectively double that figure.

If wages increase beyond inflation, prices increase, impeding demand and jobs. Also there is less money for companies to invest. Professor Patrick Minford has said: 'My estimates suggest that at rates of pay only 10% below existing market rates, unemployment would effectively disappear. In other words, 2.25 million more jobs exist at rates of pay up to 10% below the rates workers will not now willingly accept.'[13]

Pros and cons

The biggest obstacles to such a scheme are that on the one hand the Trade Unions clearly have no interest in promoting it, as such a scheme is considered to stand directly opposed to their whole reason for existence; and members of management, though perhaps intrigued by the prospects for productivity as well as any employment benefits, do not propose the idea because they are convinced that it would be unworkable and resented by the workforce.

There is however, enough evidence from the United States economy, where real wages declined during 1980–2 and job creation increased, to suggest that it is workable, even if selectively. And surely it is the responsibility of Christians to take advantage of any opportunity to help to increase the numbers of those employed. What, though, of the argument based on the precept that 'the labourer is worthy of his hire'?

It all depends on what you mean by 'hire'. I believe very much in the biblical precept, but the fact – by which Christians should be challenged – is that the worth of a worker's hire may well alter when the UK is still in an uncompetitive position in world economic terms, and when there are well over three million people unemployed. Many of those would be happy to do your job, perhaps for less money.

Ultimately, if Britain continues to allow the cost of labour to outstrip the rate of inflation-improvement or productivity-improvement, then the country will become progressively less competitive and the cost will be even fewer available jobs.

Christians have to be prepared to play a part in trying to reverse this trend. They must be prepared to be active in attempting to convince their fellow-employees and company managements of the effects of wage constraint upon the employment issue in a selfish and greedy world.

Currently there is solid evidence that pay increases are once again beginning to accelerate. Companies are demonstrating a preference for rewarding the employees that they already have, and trying to obtain further productivity increases at the wage negotiating table, rather than for holding down real wage increases and increasing employment.

So the current situation creates a wholly unjust dichotomy. On one hand, an unemployment market exists where workers are prepared to work at below the current minimum wage. On the other hand, those who *are* employed are resisting any kind of cuts and in fact frequently succeed in obtaining pay increases which exceed the rate of inflation.

Is not this diametrically opposed to the biblical principle of justice? And if it is, then should it not be combated on the shop floor, in the offices, and in the board rooms of all companies in which such a situation exists?

Providing capital for new business ventures

In the short economic history in Part 1 of this book, we suggested that one of the major problems has been the chronic decline in what has been called the entrepreneurial spirit. More simply, it could be called the decline in numbers of those starting up new businesses.

We are not talking merely about five-minute wonders, limited to short-term success followed by a speedy collapse, but about companies which start up, flourish, expand, and provide some long-term employment.

One of the principal factors in the decline of that spirit has often been the fear of having to rely on oneself, and of being forced to put everything at risk. There is all the difference in the world between a work environment where one is answerable to others, has a clear job-definition, and is paid by somebody else for work which does not relate directly to one's domestic security – and one in which the responsibility rests entirely on oneself, in which most of the hard work has to be done by oneself, and in which the failure of the business might well mean the loss of home, personal security, domestic comforts and – in a distressingly high number of cases – even one's marriage.

In the circumstances, it is not surprising that many people who might otherwise be well suited to starting their own businesses, and for whom it would mean escape from unemployment and the potential of actually becoming employers of others, lack the nerve to follow their ideas through.

Though many advisory services and finance schemes are available, ultimately the major qualifying factors in the potential success or failure of a new business are often the cost of the start-up finance, and the lack of subsequent monitoring of the business to ensure that the original plans are carried through and targets maintained.

By their nature, cashflows and projections rarely turn out to be precise, since it is impossible to forecast all the variables that may affect the business. The management of these variables, and the way that they are handled in real, practical terms, can make all the difference between success and failure.

There do exist certain grants and services in Britain, and these are listed at the end of this book; but the kind of practical help I have in mind is not really available.

Loan guarantee

Currently the Government Loan Scheme is only guaranteeing up to 70% of the loan made by the clearing banks, and costs a premium of 5% over and above the rate at which the bank might charge. This could mean that an individual is being faced with financing his start-up with money borrowed at 7%–9% above the bank's base lending rate.

Very few large, established companies would survive if they had to finance themselves at such a crippling rate of interest, let alone the small – and by definition, shaky – new business.

One of the reasons for the high cost of this money is the difficulty lenders have of distinguishing between somebody who honestly intends to make a success of his business and somebody who is simply fantasising, without the commitment to carry it through.

In the light of the many drawbacks, it is not fair for Christians to stigmatise those who shy away from starting new businesses as lacking in courage or faith. The forces working against them are very strong.

My proposal is that Christians, aware of the difficulties, should consider how those forces might be overcome, how the whole proposition of creating new businesses be made more feasible.

Private lending

In our society, most of the adult population are home-owners. Inflation in property typically far outstrips the average inflation rate. There is, consequently, a wealth of potential funding in property equity.

In biblical times, I would contend, loans for new ventures were made by the family without interest. Indeed, in the law of Moses, property and ownership was far more of a family concern than a personal one. It is quite clear that there was a very different relationship between capital and labour to that which exists today. In Old Testament times, a cornerstone of Jewish life was that sense of the whole community being bound together by the strength of family and neighbourly support in all aspects of life.

On the other hand it must be pointed out that loans in Israel were generally speaking not commercial but charitable, designed to help somebody through a difficult time, not somebody starting up a new business.

However, Deuteronomy 23:20 allows that a foreigner may be charged interest. In the contemporary extra-biblical Code of Hammurabi[1] – which is our best guide to the practice of law and order and attitude to the law in Babylon – interest is also mentioned as an established commercial practice. Indeed, Matthew 25:27 and Luke 19:23 would seem to indicate that investment to earn income commercially was not frowned upon but was normal practice. The great warnings concern the conditions of borrowing both from the point of view of the responsibility of the lender and that of the borrower. Above all, usury – lending money at extortionate rates of interest – is condemned.

In the light of such strong biblical teaching, pointing towards a use of personal wealth to help others in need while at the same time not profiting excessively from the trans-action, the existence of a substantial property equity in a society experiencing massive unemployment deserves to be re-examined.

My suggestion is that Christians should be prepared at least to consider raising money against their houses – or indeed their savings – to put up as venture capital for new businesses, either interest free or at the true cost to themselves, whichever might be appropriate.

The suggestion is a radical one, and there are many reasons why it might not be realistic or wise for a particular individual or family to adopt it. But it ought to be considered carefully before that decision is made, because somebody who owns a house or has paid off a significant part of his or her mortgage actually possesses the resources to finance new business.

A venture programme

The raising of the finance in the manner I have outlined is relatively simple and is best discussed with a banker or broker, who will advise on the practical implications and likely costings of second mortgages and loans against collateral. Naturally, any step which involves putting at risk what is for most families their biggest single capital asset, should not be undertaken without expert advice, applied to the specific circumstances of the individual case.

The greatest problem to be dealt with is that of ensuring that the money is lent responsibly. This is a task which is beyond the obligations, and indeed expertise, of most ministers, elders and deacons, though some representatives at least from these should be involved in a particular church's scheme if only as observers. The main advisory team, however, should be a team of Christian business experts, who may be co-opted from outside the church's membership. They would act as stewards of the money – by which I mean that they would keep in detailed touch with the use of the money and the progress of the business it was funding, at least on a monthly basis.

So what would a viable scheme consist of? The following elements would constitute a minimum programme.

1. Exploration of potential funds which could be made available from the church membership in the ways outlined above.

2. Encouragement of unemployed people seriously to examine the possibilities for self-employment.

3. An assessment of expertise available to the church either from its own membership or from other local experts, leading to the creation of a team of business experts qualified to appraise new business ideas presented to them. Such a team would be able to bring knowledge and experience to bear in marketing, production, development, distribution and finance in so far as such matters are relevant to the particular schemes pursued.

4. Analysis of the costs and market potential *with* the prospective entrepreneur, so that he or she learns from watching that analysis performed and understands the nature of the proposed business better thereby.

5. The production of a business 'package', which should be the first target of the programme, which would contain: the concept and philosophy of the new business; statements of how and why the proposed owners/staff are suitable candidates to run it; projected cashflows and projected profit and loss statements, together with details of how the project is to be financed.

6. Proposal of the venture by the team to the bank that they intend to use, to ascertain what degree of help can be expected from the bank (and also to obtain its independent advice as to the viability of the scheme).

7. Decisions, if the venture goes ahead, as to whether it should be a sole proprietorship, a partnership or a limited company.

8. Formalisation of who is responsible for what duties and of job definitions.

9. Finally, shareholders' agreements, bank mandates, management agreements and loan agreements should all be drawn up to make the scheme formally established.

At the end of this programme, having gone through these disciplines, everybody should be completely clear about what is involved.

Different schemes will require different approaches. However, I believe that equity and profit sharing to all working participants is a fundamental principle in running a Christian business.

Having got the enterprise going, the next important task is to monitor its progress. This should be at least a monthly exercise.

It would involve, for example, checking actual cashflow projections and profit and loss statements against the budgeted predictions. Then in the light of the new information thus gained, the forward projections could be realistically amended. The sales progress would also need to be monitored regularly. The result of regular review is that it would be relatively straightforward to take action as crises developed, rather than be faced with rescuing a company that had allowed itself to get into major difficulties. Often, the continuing success of a business depends upon how well or badly unforeseen events are dealt with.

Eventually, the loans to the business will be repaid, and the business will be self-supporting. It will generate new employment in its own right, and the original venture capital will be released so that another project can be financed.

The job saver scheme

Let us look more closely at the concept of private venture funding, for it is, I believe, a way of tackling one of the aspects of the unemployment crisis that is least talked about, that is, job scarcity through company liquidations. What follows is a description of the 'job saver' approach – the term is my own – and it is an example of how specialist gifts in the church can be put to use in helping the unemployment problem. As will be seen, this kind of scheme requires those running it to have particular skills and resources.

The impact of unemployment upon the individual, and the urgent needs that have to be met in terms of basic subsistence, human dignity and future planning are very great. The emphasis in most people's minds is on the individual, rather than the company for which he or she no longer works. And this is understandable.

However, it remains the fact that those who receive least attention in the unemployment issue are the thousands of companies that create the job losses in the first place. They fail either by being forced into liquidation by market factors or by lack of growth caused by lack of funds or management expertise.

There is considerable publicity given to the numbers of new start-up businesses; yet little attention is given to the ever-increasing numbers of businesses that go bankrupt (see page 72). These figures are ominous. For example, the main reason that the Government Loan Scheme is now so expensive is the huge number of cases where the banks have needed to take up the government guarantee because a business has failed.

How businesses fail

Of course a certain number of new businesses are doomed to failure because from the outset the concept of the business was faulty, or it was not planned properly, or there was a lack of commitment to making it work in the first place.

Many businesses are started with every intention of failure, either as outright fraud against customers, creditors or shareholders, or with a view to taxation benefits.

However, most new businesses are started with every intention on the owner's part of making them a thoroughgoing success. Failure occurs perhaps because of a bad debt, a lack of capital, inadequate marketing expertise, over-trading, bad professional advice, or slow paying customers. Problems can arise if suppliers are forced to cut their credit terms because they are themselves going through a cashflow crisis.

Sometimes it can be simply a case of interest rates rising dramatically, the cost of money soaring, and the business being unable to withstand the increased cost of its borrowing. Often premises are subject to major rent review and at the same time rates are increased, and the increased cost of overheads cannot be absorbed.

Whatever the reason, the end result is a loss of jobs and escalating unemployment problems.

In recent years business failures have been increasing at an extraordinary rate. The Department of Trade and Industry statistics[2] show the number of company liquidations as follows:

1979	1980	1981	1982	1983	1984
4,537	6,890	8,591	12,067	13,406	13,721

This represents an increase of more than 300% during the six years. These figures only relate to company failures; partnership and sole trading (one-man-businesses) operations are not included.

The stresses of failure

Money that could save these businesses and the advice that is needed to help put them back on course are both scarce commodities. Bankers tend to give favourable consideration only to schemes which are properly thought through, and this is quite understandable. But the problem is that most of those running new businesses who find themselves in the kind of difficulties we have outlined also usually have their accounts in arrears and in disarray.

They know where their major problems lie, but do not have either the knowledge or the expertise to present their problems in the form of profit and loss statements, balance sheets or cashflow analyses. They are reluctant to incur the additional costs of an accountant and, in many cases, an accountancy practice once approached is unwilling to take on the additional work for fear of the business failing and the account remaining unpaid.

At this point the bank becomes the enemy in the borrower's mind. The last thing that he wants to do is to confess how bad things really are, for fear of losing the support of the bank and possibly having the bank foreclose on its lendings. In these situations it is usually the case that borrowings for the business are secured against personal property; the thought of losing one's home is, quite naturally, unbearable.

Often the businessman lies to his wife in an attempt to escape facing up to the reality of the problem. Suppliers, customers and staff are told any plausible story that will keep the business going. The pressures mount to an intolerable level. Depression frequently follows, arguments start at home, and the marriage itself may be put at risk, divorce looming on the horizon. With the intense pressures that come from trying to keep a business afloat in these circumstances, the last thing that anybody needs is domestic pressures as well.

Meanwhile the family is left at home, aware that things have gone wrong yet unable to do anything to help except sit and take it when the husband/father comes home angry after a day of crushing strain at work. He will usually refuse to discuss any of it, preferring to sit in an armchair and sleep. When he finally goes to bed, restless nights follow the long hours of work and the tense evening. It is a pattern of depression and stress that is all too familiar in today's business climate.

It is at this point that the entrepreneur comes to the bleak realisation of the loneliness involved in running a business. As with many stress patterns, movement forward is only possible when a realistic assessment of the situation, stripped of self-deception and pretending to others, can be achieved. But, ironically, when the businessman for the first time faces up to the consequences of his own decision-making, to loss of confidence and sense of failure, the realisation often only adds to the problems and pressures.

Many people tend to label those who run their own businesses as 'get-rich-quick merchants', 'tax avoiders', 'the go-bust-and-start-all-over-again brigade', and so on. News of the collapse of their enterprises can produce a reaction almost of moral approval. But though there is an element like that –

for corruption runs through all sectors of society – the situation for the majority is as sad as I have described it.

The significance of cash

We have talked elsewhere about the sense of failure that is experienced by those who are made redundant, or have not been able to find a job. That, overwhelming as it is, however, is as nothing compared to the despair of someone who has actually started his own business, failed at it, and lost everything in the process.

That process is like the demolition of a house of cards. Remove one part of the structure, and many other cards collapse with it. For each business failure there are many bad debts, which can in their turn seriously affect the chances of survival of the suppliers' companies. The failure of one large company can frequently bring about the loss of twice as many jobs as it possessed itself, by a process of cause and effect on companies trading with it.

Some may argue that what is happening in such a case is merely a kind of 'natural selection' operating in the market place. Companies are reacting to market forces, only the strongest survive, and the weakest go to the wall.

However, apart from its intrinsic lack of compassion, this argument also suffers from a restricted definition of market strength. 'Strength' is taken to mean 'cash rich'. Yet often companies which are cash rich are only in that position because of a history of good trading. Perhaps they have wealthy backers and have succeeded in buying themselves into a near-monopoly supply situation.

But their cash riches may be the result of a failure to reinvest profits into modern plant and machinery. So the large bank balance might be an indication of a lack of good management innovation, flair and all the other ingredients that go towards making a company a good company.

Sometimes the reverse applies, and well-run companies, having flair and innovation, often go into liquidation simply because they are not cash rich. Perhaps they have been investing heavily in the future, or their companies are too young to have built up a substantial net worth. The fact remains that it is not only inept and badly managed companies that go to the wall. Good businesses can fail as well, for reasons beyond their control or sometimes because of a single error of judgement.

Clearly, if help could be given to companies facing situations like these, fewer bankruptcies would occur and as a result some impact could be made on the rising unemployment figures.

Funding growth

Similar arguments apply to businesses that would like to grow, and in growing would create further jobs, yet cannot do so because their borrowings are supposedly too high. This is not because they could not fund the increased borrowing they need – they almost certainly could. It is because the ratio of funds from shareholders to funds raised by bank borrowing is regarded as too high, and the proportion of the company's financial assets that are subject to capital repayment is felt to be unacceptably large. There are other, similar equations which are used as arguments against expansion by those who control the purse strings.

In the case of a situation such as the foregoing, it would be possible to raise more money by selling part of the owner's equity in the business; but many owners resist selling shares, which might mean losing control of their own company, just in order to fund the next step forward.

This situation cries out for venture capital funding and the kind of counselling whereby, if the accounts need doing, the consultant sits down and does the accounts; if the debtors are taking longer and longer to pay their bills, the consultant picks up the phone and chases the debts; or if sales are falling, the consultant goes out and does some face-to-face selling. But businesses who need such a service are by definition the very ones that cannot afford high consultancy fees paid speculatively, nor pay astronomically high interest on borrowings.

What is needed is a venture capital fund that is expertly administered, involving realistic interest rates, for which the investment is judged on the basis of the ultimate commercial viability of the venture, irrespective of security.

In such a fund the investment would primarily be in the integrity of the person. If he can demonstrate his total commitment to the business (a commitment which for example can be demonstrated by putting up house and other possessions as collateral against his bank borrowings), can demonstrate his skill in doing what the business exists to do in the first place (if, for example, the proprietor of a catering business is himself or herself a qualified and experienced caterer), and if he is prepared to take advice, then in most cases this should be regarded as a good potential investment of both time and money.

What we come back to is this question: What kind of resource can meet those needs?

The answer is a job saver scheme – which is what we have been describing.

Some ideas on how to start one follow.

Giving help

Arguably, a business that has already been operational can be considered a sounder investment opportunity than a new venture, because there is a financial history and the owner will have gained considerable experience of what does, and what does not, work in his business.

Most voluntary services involved in unemployment counselling spend their time and efforts on the more attractive area of trying to create new jobs. But what is often not realised is that a major effort in trying to preserve existing jobs, or helping to create new jobs by helping companies to grow, can have just as big, and possibly a bigger, impact.

So – how does one set up such a consultancy, and how does one find the companies that need help?

The answer to the latter question is simple. The need for help of this kind is so great that if a consultancy operating on these lines were to advertise for clients, businesses would beat a path to its front door.

The sums involved may often be quite small compared with

those involved in starting a new business from scratch. It may even be possible to obtain funding for this type of project from local industry, particularly in getting expert help and advice for the consultancy services required.

An organisation that should be contacted early on in setting up a scheme is Business in the Community. This operates over 200 Enterprise Agencies throughout the United Kingdom, is supported by approximately 2,500 sponsors, and is funded to the level of about £10 million per annum by business, local authorities, and central government.[3]

The aims of this network include helping create new jobs from the start-up of businesses, saving jobs in existing businesses, and expanding young companies.

The agencies act as a source of free information and advice for new and existing small businesses. They also offer business consultancy in handling accountancy, finance management, marketing and production problems. They offer training in management practices, and act as a catalyst for collaboration between private and public bodies in launching new job creation initiatives.

It may be that Business in the Community could provide advice in setting up a local job saver scheme, or it may be prepared to advise on investment opportunities. Perhaps your church can act as an additional channel for referring new clients to the agencies. Perhaps a local Christian employer would be prepared to help with setting up a new scheme, or would appreciate being put in touch with the Enterprise Agency network so that he can involve his own company.

Different churches with different resources will have different opportunities in this area. But action is certainly needed, and can make a significant contribution to alleviating the current problems.

Local bank managers can be useful in referring clients to a job saver scheme; they are encountering the sharp end of these problems in their daily work. When the scheme is working, interviews should be sought with local bank managers in order to explain the thinking and the resources that can be placed behind the idea. I am sure that many of them would be glad to let the business community know of your existence.

A CASE HISTORY

An example of job saver counselling I have come across involved the owner of a manufacturing business, who had put up everything that he owned as collateral for his company. Through no fault of his own he suffered a bad debt and could no longer raise the cash necessary to handle his future orders.

He contacted the job saver scheme when it seemed that the only outcome would be personal and business ruin for the owner and his family.

A loan of £10,000 was made using the resources of the scheme. The company is now flourishing. Its expected profits are of the order of £40,000. This reversal from financial disaster was achieved by relatively low funding, a certain amount of management consultation, renegotiation of the customer payment schedule, and some co-operation from his creditors.

Since then, the business has taken on two more employees and is set for another successful year's trading.

In another example, a small shop needed just £500 assistance and some consultation on marketing which involved a review of pricing policies and product ranges. The shop is now operating successfully.

There are numerous examples one could cite. In general they show that usually the required investments are not large and the advice given is not usually revolutionary. But the results can be staggering.

It is difficult to imagine a better manager of a business than someone who has been brought to the verge of bankruptcy and had all the benefits of the experience of his mistakes behind him. Given a second chance, he is determined never to repeat those mistakes. The money that has been lost has in fact purchased a 'learning curve' and a protection against future problems. The transaction will never appear on a balance sheet, but it is an invaluable asset for a prospective investor.

It is not necessary to have large funds in the bank to become involved in a job saver scheme. A typical group of members in many churches will have between them assets including house ownership, regular jobs and savings. By realising some of those assets jobs can be saved.

There is certainly an element of risk. The sponsors of such a scheme are investors, not savers, and there is always a risk that any investment will fail. But a well-thought-out scheme will invest wisely on the criteria already discussed; and in any case, the steward who buried his talents was strongly condemned by Jesus.

Whether your church decides to support an existing Enterprise Agency, encourages one of its members to become involved, or has the necessary expertise and resources to set up a scheme itself, investment in this area is one of the most far-reaching ways of affecting the unemployment situation.

In the end the challenge is the biblical one: to whom does our money belong? To us, or to God?

The statistics are cheerless and implacable. The only real solutions require commitment of time, talents and money.

A job saver scheme

If you have not previously thought in these terms, the whole idea might seem to be impracticable and idealistic. But it is by no means unworkable. I would like now to give an example of such a scheme which is operating successfully, and the scheme I would like to describe is my own.

Until recently, my career was like something out of a textbook. I did all the correct things and acquired all the recommended experience.

From the beginning, my ambition was to be a professionally trained managing director. I took the normal route; a successful period in sales, then sales training, then a public relations post with a large corporation. This was followed by a period of projects in production, quality control, and computerisation; after which I was off to the Harvard Business School, graduated, ran a small division of a major company, then held a large materials management job, then my first chief executive job (running a group of businesses for a multi-national), then my first chief executive post in a public company, then the multi-business chief executive post, then the multi-national chief executive post, then the standard heart operation.

Lying in hospital, in a considerably weakened state, I wondered what course my life should take now. Things would certainly have to be different.

As I contemplated the future, I began to think about the unemployment problem. For many years I had been deeply interested in the subject. I had made a major study of it. I had given talks to Chambers of Commerce, Confederation of British Industry and British Institute of Management meetings, and to various church groups.

Perhaps my future career could involve answering some of the practical questions that the unemployment issue had given me in the past. Certainly the plan uppermost in my mind was to leave the ranks of those working for large corporations, and branch out on my own. If that could go hand in hand with creating new employment, so much the better.

I decided to look for ways in which I could implement the ideas which I had been developing, many of which are now contained in this book. Eventually I made the decision to enter the world of subcontracting.

My assets were my house, my experience in management, and some money. When I was out of hospital and fit, I went to see my bank manager for a preliminary discussion of the various possibilities of raising capital, within the constraints of my assets and the viability of my ideas. Having done so, I looked for a place to begin.

The event that became the starting point of my new career was a meeting with somebody who shared an enthusiasm of my own; the idea of selling companies a service which would make use of the expertise of the unemployed – to do jobs which were best done outside the normal organisational structures, which were affected by seasonal shortages or staff absences, or which created special staffing problems. Indeed, any problem which could be solved by the management of labour, would come within the scope of the scheme.

The person concerned had the necessary expertise, knowledge of the employment market, much energy and enthusiasm, but no capital. It seemed an ideal partnership.

I researched the cost of premises, selling costs and administrative expenses. I calculated the rates of pay that would have to apply and the potential billings that could be charged to clients. Then, armed with a worked-out business plan, I offered the bank my first investment proposal.

The scheme was well received. However, my professional advisors were taken aback by one stipulation. I insisted that the staff of the new enterprise should have a controlling financial interest in it. I wanted them to have a majority shareholding.

I pointed out why I wanted this. I was contributing one ingredient; capital and the management of the books. But all the other factors which would determine whether the business was a success or a failure were being supplied by the workers.

Once this was resolved, the business was set up as I had requested.

Almost immediately, it became successful. Unfortunately, my plans to repeat the same formula elsewhere were thwarted by a number of factors, none of which was under my control. Since the return on the investment in that one business was not enough to support my family, and since it was not my intention to draw more than a nominal salary from the business for managing the accounts, I would have to look elsewhere for an income.

It came in an unexpected way. I began to receive telephone calls from the managers of small businesses, asking for help and advice. These businesses were only one or two years old and were having considerable difficulty in surviving.

Almost unrealised at first, a new consultancy was being born.

I decided that the terms of this consultancy would be as follows. If I could not solve a business's financial and management problems, I would charge nothing. If, however, I was successful, I would charge a reasonable fee.

Word of the new consultancy was passed around, and within months I had nine clients. I was dealing with businesses as diverse as an automation manufacturing business, a garage, an advertising agency, a coffee shop, and a bathroom fitting business. So the consultancy developed.

I came to realise that in the present period, when more businesses are going into liquidation in this country than ever before, there was just as important a task to be done in preserving (and creating jobs in) what were ailing businesses as there was in generating new businesses. I coined a name for that task: 'job stewardship'.

Since that time, my original scheme – the new business ventures – has developed and expanded. There are now three, with another planned. The consultancy has also grown, to the extent that I am now employing somebody to help me with the accountancy work.

The new businesses now employ about 110 people, and the consultancy has preserved some 130 jobs, in six months of operation.

None of the businesses receives subsidies, either from charities or government aid programmes. They stand on their own feet and compete successfully in the open market place. The jobs are therefore real jobs, and I would expect them to be there in years to come.

I now sit on the board of a venture capital company, and of a company that specialises in raising funds through public and institutional investors. This expands the opportunities for providing more money for new business start-ups, or occasionally for businesses in trouble.

The decision to embark on these ventures demanded a great act of faith, from my wife especially and also from my children.

However, there are benefits to my family. Because of the way the work is structured, minimal time is expended on cost controls because the staff, being majority shareholders, are, in effect, spending their own money. Of course guidance is needed from time to time, but a system of planned visits works well. Similarly, the work of the consultancy can be planned ahead, except where crises develop, as they do from time to time.

The result is that I am able to spend more time working

from an office at home and enjoying the fruits of family life which, in my previous hectic lifestyle, I usually missed.

I realise, of course, that no two people are the same; but I believe that there are many people who have the same opportunity to use the talents and resources that they have for the creation and preservation of real jobs.

Despite my intense interest in the unemployment issue, it took a period in hospital to force me to take stock of what I was doing – or rather, not doing – about it.

When I refrain from doing something that God is calling me to do because of fear or uncertainty, risk, or financial loss, it is as if I have actually taken personal part ownership of part of God's creation, instead of realising my stewardship responsibilities. It is as if I am not willing to depend on him to provide, as if I have given to myself such talents as I possess, as if everything that I have done has been carried through by my own strength and initiative.

Any form of stewardship involves care in spending our time, talents and money. I feel that there can be no better way of using them than in working to overcome an evil, such as unemployment, which opposes all biblical precepts and teaching.

Whether time, talents and money are deployed in part-time or full-time service – for example in a project such as I have described – is a matter for each individual to decide between himself and God.

But one thing is certain. To pronounce revulsion and abhorrence for something that is clearly dehumanising and wrong, while at the same time doing absolutely nothing to help to overcome it, is surely a flat contradiction of all that the Bible teaches.

Work sharing in a climate of de-manning

In recent years Britain has undergone a period of severe 'de-manning'. Voluntary redundancy agreements have been an attractive proposition for many workers. Some have left and have not been replaced. In some cases companies have restructured their workforce to allow for a more efficient use of smaller numbers.

Now that the economy shows signs of restabilising, the reaction of many employers is to resist increasing their workforce back to the sort of size it was before the current crisis.

It is a natural reaction, even though business may be picking up and the economic prospects looking distinctly favourable. Quite apart from the emotional stress that hiring and firing causes for both employee and employer, the process is also uneconomic and in fact is extremely costly. Hence there has been a tendency to look at ways of coping with the increased workload, while at the same time avoiding further labour costs and commitments.

Traditionally, this has been achieved by using overtime. This is a popular method with employers and employees, even though in real terms if often carries an additional cost of between a third and double the cost of labour. The employee is pleased to have an opportunity to increase his wage packet; the employer is satisfied because he has increased output without the risks and problems that go with hiring extra staff.

In one sense, overtime promotes the philosophy of maintaining full employment within a company. But at the same time, it generates an element of unrealism. Employees can easily reach a point where overtime is so much a part of the normal working week that what was originally a 'bonus' in the pay packet becomes a normal part of the weekly earnings. The employee depends on this element, and it can even become a factor in pay bargaining – for example, guaranteed overtime might be a negotiating condition. At that point, overtime is no longer something which is introduced as a temporary solution to short-term workflow crises – it has become an intrinsic part of the employment structure.

At home, the family gets used to the odd hours kept by its major earner, on the assumption that the inconvenience is a reasonable trade-off against a better standard of living. In the workplace, the company accepts increased labour costs on the grounds that they are part of the price to be paid for maintaining a philosophy of full employment and a well-paid staff.

Yet there is a problem here, for such a situation stands completely opposed to what the Bible teaches. Is it right to work longer and earn more when your fellow man is unemployed and earns nothing? Clearly the concept of sharing the work (skills and experience permitting) with a member of the unemployed is a much more desirable situation, and we will next consider some of the ways in which this can be achieved.

The Job Splitting and Phased Retirement Schemes

Interestingly enough, out of all the present government work-creation schemes currently operating, it is the Job Splitting Scheme that has had the least 'take-up'. The scheme was introduced in January 1983, and in essence it pays a company £750 pa if a job – and its pay – is shared between two people, one of whom is recruited from the unemployed. The scheme actually costs the government virtually nothing, as the cost is offset by the savings in unemployment benefits.

The Job Splitting Scheme has certain advantages in that it enables an older, more experienced person to pass on his or her knowledge to a new recruit. It also automatically increases cover for holidays, sickness, or an increase in the work rate, as either party can work voluntary overtime and is indeed often in a position to do so. For people approaching retirement, or women who want to spend more time with their families while not leaving the work environment entirely (for financial or social reasons), the scheme could be very attractive.

A complementary scheme for older employees introduced in October 1983 is the Phased Retirement Scheme. An employee aged 62 or older is entitled to half the Job Release Scheme allowance if he or she works half-time up to retirement, thus allowing an additional person to be recruited half-time. The only difference between the two schemes – apart from age – is that the former provides a subsidy to the employer, and the latter to the employee.

In both schemes, the underlying principle is that those who have work should be prepared to share their good fortune with the unemployed.

Work sharing and new jobs

There is a good case, as we have just seen, for examining work sharing schemes in relation to jobs that are already in existence. Even more attractive, and much easier to implement, are similar schemes in situations where new jobs are being created.

In such circumstances the employer benefits in several ways.

1. In jobs where there are 'peaks and troughs' of activity, working hours are made much more flexible by work sharing, and it is quite possible to have the working hours overlapping, thereby virtually doubling the workforce at times of maximum workload.

2. Illness and holidays are better covered, with considerable opportunity for one employee to stand in for another on a temporary basis.

3. If one member of the workforce leaves, another is available to do the extra work on a temporary basis – and that person will need no training or 'settling-in time', as he or she is already doing the job.

4. Flexibility in working hours reduces the unavoidable reasons for employees' absence from work – many domestic commitments (doctor, dentist, waiting for the gas man etc.) can be rescheduled out of the employee's working hours.

5. There is a bonus in productivity. A study was undertaken in 1981 by Eduard Gaugler at Mannheim University[4] on the effects of job sharing experiments in the Rhine area. It showed that the job sharers' productivity was some 33% higher than that of full-time workers.

6. This method offers greater potential resources for career development.

It is true that there are some disadvantages. These include, for example:

1. The scheduling of working hours in relation to work requirements.

2. The need to ensure that the disciplines of work 'handovers' are properly managed.

3. Funding the extra costs of training (two people have to be trained for each job).

However, given the right application, the benefits far outweigh the disadvantages. In 1981 *International Management* conducted a survey on alternative work patterns in ten Western European countries. It showed that 11% of those companies surveyed had tried job sharing, and that a further 8% had plans to try within the next five years. Of the companies which had tried the scheme, 27% planned to extend the programme, 62% planned to maintain it at existing levels, and only 7% had dropped or planned to drop the programme (the remainder, 4% of those who had tried job sharing, did not provide further details).[5]

Such results speak for themselves. Few companies have attempted job sharing schemes; but of those who have, 88% are either keeping the schemes or expanding them.

There are fundamental issues raised here which are relevant to the well-being of companies and of individuals. Job sharing is compatible with efficiency, cost-competitiveness – and with biblical teaching! There is an urgent need to discuss the whole matter with companies at whatever level access exists – whether it be an individual employee raising it directly with his or her employer, a Trade Union putting the matter on the table during routine discussions with management, or a suggestion at board-room level by means of discussion between companies and through organisations such as the Confederation of British Industry.

Job sharing is not a revolutionary answer to our problems, and it is not the whole solution to them. But it would certainly make a difference, in terms of corporate efficiency, the national economy and – for want of a better phrase – the national morale.

Why then has it not been more widely adopted?

The obstacles are the old, familiar ones: employer inertia, rooted in cultural preconditions about what is possible or desirable; and employee inertia, rooted in fixed ideas about what is the proper way to discharge an individual's responsibilities within society – the notion that only a 40-hour working week is a 'proper job'.

But the obligation remains for the individual Christian and the Church; to encourage employers to investigate closely more flexible work patterns, with a view to assessing how putting them into practice might have substantial benefits in the whole area of work creation and helping the unemployed.

How to become a government agent

Besides the initiatives documented in the earlier chapters of this book, there are many other schemes in which churches can jointly or independently become involved.

It is fairly well known that the Manpower Services Commission (MSC) runs many government-funded schemes, such as the Youth Training Scheme (YTS), the Young Workers Scheme (YWS – this has very little voluntary participation, so is outside the scope of the present book) and the Community Programme (CP). However, it is not commonly understood how these schemes operate in practice, and the part that the churches can play in organising themselves to participate in them, so making a contribution to the solving of their local unemployment problems.

To a large extent the government-funded schemes depend on local agencies through which they can operate. The agencies can seek out and define the local need, and identify what resources exist to meet those needs within criteria laid down by the MSC.

In many cases links between the church and the MSC can work very well, since on the one hand the church has a pastoral role in the community and is therefore well placed to find appropriate schemes; and on the other, while it is often keen to assist with the unemployment problem, it may have insufficient funds to do all the things it wants to.

To help churches interested in looking at what is involved in such a collaboration, I list below some of the government schemes in operation, and describe how they operate and what sort of role a local church might have.

Opportunities for volunteering

This scheme is funded by the Department of Health and Social Security to enable grants to be made to voluntary organisations for helping unemployed people to undertake voluntary work in the fields of health and social services.

In 1984/5 some £5 million has been allocated to support more than 550 projects. Grants for capital purposes are limited to £15,000 for any one project, and out-of-pocket expenses may be paid to volunteers. The scheme is administered currently by a number of agencies including a consortium of seven national voluntary organisations.

Some 7,200 unemployed volunteers are participating.

The scheme is operated in Wales by the Wales Council for Voluntary Action; in Scotland, advice on the scheme can be obtained from the Volunteer Development Scotland Office.

The Youth Training Scheme

This scheme is open only to 16-year-old school leavers and some 17-year-olds. The scheme is intended to provide these people with 12 months' experience of work in order to help them make a successful transition from school to the working environment, and as a result make them, in the eyes of a potential employer, more capable of contributing to an organisation.

All YTS schemes must provide the young person with a detailed training programme in the following basic skills: numeracy, communication, problem solving and planning, manual dexterity and computer literacy. The training programme will involve both exposure to these areas at the workplace, and a minimum of 13 weeks in the 12-month programme in off-the-job training at a college or similar establishment.

The scheme must also provide the young person with an awareness of the importance of each individual's work effort, how that combines to produce a company result, and how the company operates in relation to other industries. It must also offer training in a specific job skill, as well as training in flexibility and adaptability of that skill in different work environments. Each scheme should provide a proper induction to the training programme, and to the organisation that the trainee will be working in. There should be regular assessment, guidance and support for each trainee, so that progress can be reviewed and recorded.

These criteria are common to all YTS schemes. There are three 'modes' of operation.

'Mode A'　This mode of operation is typically that run by employers who are individual companies, or by 'managing agents' – these may be local trade associations, Chambers of Commerce, consortia of small employers or large private employers.

Grants are made available to these 'sponsors', as they are called. Out of the grants, the trainee is paid a fixed weekly training allowance. In this mode, the required off-the-job training may be provided by the sponsor, or it can contract with an outside organisation to provide it.

'Mode B'　This is similar to Mode A, except that though on-the-job training is conducted by the sponsor, the scheme is linked to a training college or similar institution for off-the-job training. The MSC pays the sponsor a negotiated fee, and the trainee may be paid by the sponsor or directly by the MSC, according to arrangement.

'Mode B1'　This mode is the one that is most relevant to voluntary organisations. It falls into three categories.

1. YTS Community Projects

This can involve trainees in working on projects that benefit the community, and *any organisation or individual can apply to sponsor a YTS Community Project*. The MSC will fund the trainee's weekly allowances in full; and the Commission will also pay the wages of adult supervisors (these wages must be agreed with the MSC in advance). Sponsors may even receive further grants toward any additional operating costs such as the provision of tools, equipment or other capital items.

It will be immediately recognised that this scheme offers an attractive opportunity to a group such as a church, which often has a considerable commitment to action but does not have the kind of guaranteed regular income necessary to support a scheme for a realistic period of time.

COMMUNITY PROJECTS: AN EXAMPLE

In 1980, the men's committee of Stockton Heath Methodist Church decided to look at ways of expressing their Christian witness by tackling the unemployment problem in their area of Warrington. They had heard that a scheme was operating in Sheffield, and decided to visit it and investigate the possibilities. By the end of 1981, they had embarked on their own scheme.

The Methodist Church acts as sponsors, and the management committee of seven now includes an Anglican minister and a Baptist minister. The training that this scheme offers includes working with luncheon clubs for the elderly, playgroups, primary schools, old people's homes, and centres for the mentally handicapped.

The jobs are organised with the help of local Social Services and Roman Catholic primary schools. There are fifteen trainees, two paid supervisors and an unpaid supervisor.

2. Training workshops

Although the same criteria apply as to all other YTS schemes, the main aims of training workshops are to operate in a workshop environment and to produce goods or provide services.

Of course, such a scheme must be very carefully designed so as not to put existing businesses or jobs at risk, defeating the whole purpose of the enterprise. However, it can cover a very wide range of activities, depending on the skills locally available. Schemes are operating in areas as diverse as computer maintenance and knitwear manufacturing.

As with community projects, any organisation or group may sponsor a training workshop. The funding covers the same areas as the community projects YTS, except that the MSC covers only 90% of the agreed capital costs, subject to limits calculated according to the number of places the scheme is designed to provide. The sponsors are expected to make some contribution to the capital costs; however, they may be eligible for further funding from local authority grants or grants from similar institutions.

It is not intended that the workshops should be financially self-sufficient – at least initially – but any forecast income is deductible from the MSC grant aid.

A CASE HISTORY

The St John's Training Workshops in Grimsby were started in a climate of growing concern about the rising employment in the city. The workshops began with local parish help when a redundant church was offered to the South Humberside Industrial Mission. The organisation involved an Industrial Training Chaplain, local clergy and lay people, businessmen, trade unionists and the local Member of Parliament. Today the six members of the executive meet monthly and run what is now a large enterprise.

Its products are now exported as far afield as the Gulf States, Canada and the USA. It provides youth training, entirely in house, for 100 young people. The trainees work in groups of no more than eight and are given training as they produce goods.

Over fourteen skills are taught, including audio-visual work, building and maintenance, canteen and catering, electronics, computing, market gardening, metalwork, needlework, office work, printing, pottery, reception, stationery, site servicing and stores and woodwork. The site currently has five computers, and every trainee undergoes a computer literacy course.

The scheme has been outstandingly successful. Consistently half the trainees, on finishing the scheme, go on to find a permanent job.

Following the considerable success of this project, the entire diocese decided to expand into a diocese-wide commitment to participation in the Community Programme, which we will describe later. There are now six community programme agencies operating, and they employ some 800 people.

The Rev Canon John Rhodes, MBE, who has been very much the driving force in this venture, tells me that he is now envisaging moving on, to start a further phase to the programme by looking at how to start generating new businesses which will provide a longer-term solution.

3. Information Technology Centres

As its name implies, this scheme is very similar to the training workshops, except its prime emphasis is on training for a range of adaptable skills in the new technology.

The scheme would expect to provide at least an introduction to computer programming, word processing, computer maintenance, digital technology, control systems and electronics, together with some experience of producing high-technology products. In addition to MSC funding, the Department of Trade and Industry provides some additional assistance for capital equipment and topping up supervisory salaries.

Helping hands

It will be seen that the YTS programmes offer many opportunites for projects designed to provide work for the unemployed. There are churches participating in these schemes, ranging from million-pound projects to relatively small schemes; but the Church has not by any means taken a leading role in this field nationally.

There is a good deal of help available. Organisations exist to give specialist assistance to YTS sponsors. The Community Projects Foundation offers help in developing MSC applications for funding and setting up schemes, as well as practical advice. The Information Technology Consultancy Unit also provides information and assistance for those wishing to sponsor Information Technology Centres. The National Council for Voluntary Organisations is also available, to provide information and support to prospective sponsors on the YTS Community Programme. So the lead has been given, and the support and help is available, to any who wish to pursue a ministry in this critical area.

The Community Programme

The aim of this MSC programme is to help those who are 18 or older and have been unemployed for some time, by offering temporary jobs on projects, undertaking work which benefits the community.

As with the other schemes, *any organisation or group of individuals may act as project sponsors*. Again, care must obviously be taken to ensure that the projects are original, new, and will not take work away from other employers who are already operating. That would be subsidised competition, and it would be grossly unfair and also counter-productive in the very work that the programme is concerned with – the provision of jobs.

The range of activities can be very diverse; for example, providing social amenities or services, or improving the environment, or energy conservation – all of which benefit the community.

If the workers are aged 18 to 24, they must be receiving benefit and have been unemployed for six months or more to join the scheme. Those over 25 must have been unemployed for twelve months or more.

Each job funded by the Community Programme will allow the sponsor to claim the following: wages for the workers at the current MSC agreed level, Employers National Insurance contributions and superannuation where applicable, and an agreed annual allowance to cover the overheads of operating the scheme.

As with the YTS, organisations exist to help you become a sponsor. Details of how to contact the local Community Programme Link Team or other Community Programme Managing Agents are given at the end of this book.

A CASE HISTORY

In April 1983 the Passionist Fathers of Consett, County Durham, established a Community Programme Agency in renovated buildings in the monastery grounds. The agency had agreement for 200 places to be made available for schemes throughout Durham County. The schemes could be divided broadly between those involving environmental and building restoration work, and those of a social and community nature.

The agency is sponsoring a Community Development Project in two villages in County Durham, including a gardening and decorating scheme to help the elderly and handicapped, a welfare advice service, and a team of research and community workers who are involved in furthering the development of the local community. It is also refurbishing a derelict building in one of the villages, to be used as a resource and activity centre. Other projects include a historical research centre, a religious education resource centre, and a community development centre for the deaf.

Workers in the environmental and restoration schemes have so far constructed a children's playground, created a picnic area, and undertaken various building and decorating projects for churches and community groups. In addition the agency is now working closely with the Millhill Fathers, and has established a gardening and workshop scheme for disabled people.

Many other churches have also taken initiatives. Church Action with the Unemployed (CAWTU) has published details of 100 projects in *Action on Unemployment*.[6]

It is true to say that the MSC now has many agencies appointed to handle their YTS programme. It may be, therefore, that in your locality those needs are already taken care of satisfactorily. But under the Community Programme, considerable scope for development still exists nationwide. If you feel that taking on an agency under the programme is too great a commitment, consider contacting an existing local agency and make a start by proposing projects and asking the existing agency to manage them for you.

I have mentioned real-life examples of churches that have in various ways applied themselves to tackling the real problems. They have done as the Bible demands; they have offered time, money and talents in a particular way, to the glory of God.

The schemes are real and the opportunities are real. The Christian in the pew can have a real impact, assuming that he is prepared to devote the necessary energy and thinking time.

The pastoral support of the unemployed

In any practical programme of action to help those who are unemployed, one of the major priorities must be the pastoral needs of those whom we are trying to help. In this section we will be looking both at those needs, and at some very practical ways in which immediate and useful help can be given on a one-to-one basis and as an outworking of the Church's pastoral concern for those among whom it lives and serves.

All pastoral problems have one thing in common. The key to being able to help lies in the ability to identify with the person or persons involved. A good counsellor is only secondarily a good speaker. Primarily, he or she is a good listener.

This does not mean that one needs to have been unemployed before one can help an unemployed person, any more than it is necessary to be homeless in order to find somebody a flat. But it does mean that a clear understanding of the problems is essential – which is why a large part of this book is concerned with presenting the unemployment picture clearly and explaining the implications of the familiar statistics.

All counselling situations are different, even when the problem area is the same, because people are different and so are their circumstances.

However, this section will attempt to describe the common ground and give some constructive advice to those who are involved in giving pastoral support to the unemployed. It may also be a stimulus to some who may wish to consider being trained in this field.

Work and the time dimension

It does not need a Gallup Poll to estimate that the average working person sleeps for about eight hours a day, works for about eight hours, and plays for about eight hours. Work, for the employed, occupies some 50% of their waking moments for five days of the week.

The pattern of the week is usually set by the work we do. It determines what time we get up, eat breakfast, leave home, and return home (often tired). Work determines, negatively, how much time we have left to devote to the family before bed time; and weekends are two days without work.

For those who share their lives with others, the time dimension of work is so important that it also affects the daily routine of all the other people involved. The schedule of those working affects when the bathroom is free in the morning, when breakfast is eaten, and what time the evening meals are eaten. When factors such as overtime or particularly busy or slack periods are involved, the impact is even greater. For many people, and especially those who are unmarried, the domestic and social timetable can be totally determined by the work environment, since work can even become the centre of one's social life.

Work, in summary, has such an important role in our society that it determines most of the timetables and routines round which much of our lives are led.

Work and authority

At work, one is usually part of an organisation. In most work environments factors such as authority, discipline, social hierarchy and timetable of events are already highly structured. Often on entering work one even acquires, through Trade Union membership, a package of loyalties and tradition.

All this frequently has the effect of generating a fictitious sense of status, depending on how the employer regards the employee, and this in turn can lead many people into a false sense of security, aware of what is expected of them and believing that so long as they work within the known structures of their workplace they will be 'safe'.

Work and money

Work also affects one's life in another way; it is the way one earns net disposable income. For most employed people, the money they have in their bank account or in their pocket comes directly as a result of the work they do.

That money is usually more than they would get on unemployment benefit or supplementary benefit, and to a major extent it determines the externals of their lifestyle.

For most people, the wage packet determines the kind of house they live in, the food they eat, the clothes they wear and the possessions they own. It is also for many the major influence on how their leisure time is spent and the holidays they have; and money determines how they work on the house, work in the garden, prepare food, make clothes, buy clothes, watch TV or video, go to the theatre, study, read and so on. All these activities are affected by money; the well-paid may cut their lawn with a hover mower while their less well-paid neighbours use an old hand model, and the very well-paid will have the option of hiring somebody to mow the lawn for them.

For those living with others, the influence of earnings spreads through the household. The contribution of the sole breadwinner is self-evident. With husband and wife earning, the combined wage packets make a difference to the domestic environment, as does the contribution of a son or daughter at work.

We live in a society that is highly acquisitive and consumerised. The net disposable income dramatically affects the use of time in a family, and can reflect its social status.

Work and self-worth

If one were to attempt to collate all the prevailing cultural and social attitudes towards work into one single statement, I suspect that the statement, looking at our society, would be this: 'A man is his work'.

Self-esteem is often received through work. So ingrained is this today that often one of the first things that a person asks a stranger as a conversation starter is, 'And what do you do for a living?' – or, depending on circumstances, 'What does your wife [or daddy, or mummy] do?'

The answer is then used as the basis for a whole range of assumptions which the questioner begins to make. The stranger's level of initiative, standard of living, social class, acceptability and many other qualities are estimated. Underlying all this is the notion that having made this snap appraisal – on the basis of one answer to one question – the questioner can then move on to find some areas of common ground on which a relationship can be founded.

Such interrogations can put great pressure on families, as for example when they move house and meet their new neighbours, or when they meet colleagues from work in a social environment such as a staff party. Sometimes whole families live out a kind of role play, based on how they think society perceives the husband's job. A child may try to act in a way that he thinks is obligatory for a managing director's son, and a wife might dress in ways she does not particularly like in order to conform to her stereotyped image of what she should look like as his consort.

And so the sense of self-worth that the job gives the employee affects his whole family as well as himself. The social acceptability of wife and children becomes intricately bound in with the social acceptability of the husband's (or father's) job.

Obviously many of these attitudes are quite wrong biblically when viewed in the light of such passages as discussed in p. 6 ff. But they are nevertheless accurate reflections of how society views work.

Let us then turn the picture on its head, and consider how each of these areas is affected by joblessness.

Unemployment and the time dimension

One of the very first casualties when a person is or becomes unemployed is the complete destruction of time and routine. The main reason for doing anything within certain time frames is gone. Getting up, eating meals, dressing to go out, and any number of other parts of the pattern of the worker's day need not now be done at a particular time, or even at all.

The disruption is as catastrophic for the other members of the household as it is for the person who is jobless. When you have been in work for any length of time, adapting to other people's priority structures is a most difficult thing to do, and it almost always causes major disruption. It is a rather more serious version of the lostness that many people feel on retirement, as they look for reasons to live a structured day. But at least, in their case, they have lived out a useful life in the workplace. It is very different if that working life has been arbitrarily cut short or, indeed, has never begun.

Unemployment and authority

With all the props of imposed hierarchical structures gone, and nobody to be responsible to or for, the tendency is to over-impose similar systems in the home. A worker who has been in charge of a team and is now jobless will often attempt to relate to his family in the same way, and become dictatorial and demanding. Often he or she will intrude into the partner's sphere of authority; for example, a father will become overbearingly aggressive about shopping, or attempt to organise his wife's housekeeping as if she were a junior in the firm's stores department.

The result is that the established authority structures of the home are changed. The family begins to feel insecure, and often there are bitter arguments.

Unemployment and money

It is a sad reflection upon our society, that we have become obsessed with consumerism. Often we mark our progress through life as movement through an enormous shopping list, and when the means of feeding our acquisitiveness is taken away, all that is left is discontent, resentment and stress.

The effects of this loss are not limited to the person who is unemployed. The whole family is affected. The social exercise of shopping becomes curtailed. School trips become unafford-able. Perhaps some possessions have to be disposed of. The family car may have to go. The impact of unemployment is immediate and wide ranging. The entire family has to rebudget.

Unemployment and self-worth

An attitude still exists – a legacy and influence from the 'Victorian work ethic' – that those who have no job are pitiable, or shirkers, or weak, or disobedient to God, or lazy . . . in other words they are, in some way or other, inadequate.

Being categorised by people on the basis of the job one does is bad enough; but to be prejudged, on the criteria above, because one has no job at all, is almost unbearable.

It is as hard for a wife to admit that her husband has no job, as it is for the husband himself; and for a child to admit that his or her 'hero' has been a failure in any way at all can be a quite traumatic experience for that child.

What a terrible reflection on our social attitudes, that anybody should feel compelled to assess his self-worth and self-esteem by the job he has or has not got! It simply serves to demonstrate how far we have fallen from what God intends us to be.

Our self-worth and self-esteem are really determined on totally different criteria. To feel personal inadequacy just because one has lost one's job is to have misunderstood what life is really about. But it is not always easy to keep one's world view straight, when all the structures of daily life have suddenly been threatened by the trauma of job loss, or when months and years of unemployment have taken their toll.

The call to pastoral love

When Paul wrote to the church in Thessalonika, 'If anyone will not work, let him not eat' (2 Thess 3:10), he was talking to the voluntary unemployed, not the involuntary unemployed.

But the verse has stuck in the memory of many who have not read it carefully in context, and there has been a tendency not only to encourage industrious effort but also at the same time to despise those who are losers in the struggle for survival.

There are some people who shirk the biblical challenge to work and provide for their families. There were people like that in Thessalonika, and there are some like that in modern Britain; and there is no doubt that if Paul were writing today he would express himself in precisely the same way.

But the great majority of the unemployed are honestly anxious to work. They are victims, not of their own laziness, but of the economic system.

What should our attitude as Christians be to them?

Most importantly, we should reject any sense of superiority. Not to do so would in any case divide churches, for most have a number of unemployed members, and to categorise them as in any way less than those who are employed is to drive a wedge between members of the Body of Christ.

We should be to them as we should be to any body of suffering people. We should welcome them in our fellowship; and we should try to understand the seriousness of their problem.

Our calling is to give whatever help we can, in time, talents and money; and to translate into direct action the biblical commands concerning stewardship and giving help to those who have fallen on hard times. Passages such as Amos 8:4-6, Jesus' parables of the Good Samaritan (Luke 10:25 ff), and the Old Testament codes of compassion to one's neighbours (eg Deuteronomy 15:7 ff) are all relevant here.

Counselling: the Church's role

The loss of a job has considerable similarity to bereavement, both so far as the unemployed person is concerned and for the concerned onlookers.

For the person who has lost his or her job, the immediate reaction is a sense of shock, followed by optimism, followed by acute depression, followed by pessimism and then, at the end, fatalism.

For the concerned onlooker, there is an immediate sense of sympathy and desire to help; but once the funeral is over, the bereaved person is often left to his own devices. Anyone who has been involved with a bereavement will know that the worst times often come some six months later. Much the same pattern applies to job loss.

The parallel may seem shocking if you have never considered it before. But it certainly highlights the fact that the counselling needs of the unemployed are highly specific and reflect real emotional damage.

Without doubt, counselling the unemployed is a practical way of expressing love and concern. But it also calls for a certain level of professionalism. Churches should consider whether any of their members might be prepared to develop such skills, and perhaps be prepared to go on courses in order to provide that kind of service in their local community.

Similarly, churches should certainly consider the uses to which their buildings are put. Even the most active of churches rarely use their building resources to the full during the day. Would it not be truly glorifying to God if those premises could be adapted in some way for use as a 'pastoral centre', where the unemployed could be counselled? This would maximise the use of resources, and it would demonstrate the relevance of the Christian gospel to the problems of the present time.

Counselling guidelines

Having argued the case for churches to become involved with the pastoral care of the unemployed, I would like to conclude this section with some practical guidelines for those who take up this role. Those who are not trained counsellors should not feel that they cannot help, but it is vitally important for all who are counsellors that they commit time and emotional resources to the task. This is not like mowing the churchyard or arranging the flowers in church. You cannot be an effective counsellor simply by setting aside a couple of hours a week.

What, then, are the counselling needs of the unemployed?

We have already seen that one of the effects of being unemployed is that it can sap a person's confidence and destroy morale.

Rule number one, therefore, is *encourage continuously*. Criticism, no matter how well meant, simply increases the sense of insecurity.

Rule number two is *remember that the jobless person has a lot to contend with*. Pastoral support is therefore going to involve long periods of sympathetic listening to the person's money troubles, family problems job-hunting problems, rejection by friends and so on.

Avoid continuously asking 'How's the job-hunting going?' While this is a reasonable question from the asker's point of view and seems a useful ice-breaker, having to tell the enquirer that no job has been found just rubs salt into the wounds. If the person gets a job, he will be only too glad to tell you.

Be watchful for the signs of the all-too-frequent side effects of unemployment; marriage breakdown, lethargy, drinking, gambling and general boredom. Some of these may require specialist counselling, and it is helpful to have ready the names of sympathetic experts who are willing to involve themselves in this work, so that if help is asked for the person can be referred to an appropriate counsellor.

Involve the immediate family as much as possible in the counselling, especially the wife or husband. Similarly, if the unemployed person is a youngster living at home, the parents should be involved, so as to ensure support and understanding. In this way, all parties can air their grievances in a neutral situation. This has the advantage of getting tensions out into the open without precipitating a family argument and all the trauma and conflict that involves.

The object of counselling should be not only to air and resolve any emotional problems which unemployment may have caused, but also to work out with both husband and wife an agreed plan of 'things to be done', so that both can resolve together to tackle the problem.

Persuading both parties to work together in a combined effort can lead to a strong sense of unity in the face of unemployment, and to mutual understanding rather than to friction and possibly separation. All too often, when communication breaks down, there can be a failure to recognise each other's problems. The criticisms and accusations of selfishness and inadequacy which each levels at the other can lead to the breakdown of the marriage.

The alternative is to bind the partnership together with a sense of common purpose. We have already discussed the importance of reinforcement and encouragement, but it is far more effective when the support comes from one's own close family. The counsellor can help to bring about such a situation. In families where the wounds of unemployment have inflamed deeper problems, his or her role can be crucial.

More detailed considerations

Most people's first reaction on losing a job is shock. It can express itself in anger, despair, controlled silence or even effusive talk.

The second reaction is the fear of having to tell the family, and the expectation that the family will regard the loss of work as irresponsible, and evidence of an inability to support them. At the very least, it will mean a reduction in their value as a father or mother.

The next reaction is also one of fear: fear at the thought of the reaction of one's fellow workers. The ghastly ritual that must be gone through of clearing one's desk or locker in front of one's colleagues is the next hurdle.

It is a tragedy that at the very moment when the person needs all his wits about him, emotionally he is least able to deal with the situation. Once again, the similarity to bereavement is clear. And, as in a bereavement situation, there are certain practical steps which have to be taken, and in which help can be given by sympathetic onlookers. It is here that the counsellor can be of immediate practical help.

CHECK LISTS

The following is a list of things which should be done as soon as possible.

1. Make sure that the circumstances of the individual's dismissal are committed to writing.

2. Get the person to obtain a written statement, detailing how the financial settlement of his employment contract

has been calculated – including holiday pay, pension rights etc.

3. Make sure that before he leaves his job he receives his P45 form and any sums which may be due to him.

4. When all the above documents are assembled, the package should be taken to an expert representative – that is, a union representative or a lawyer; and make sure that the person has been treated justly and fairly.

5. Ensure that the person registers immediately for benefit with the local Unemployment Benefit Office.

6. See that he discusses the financial circumstances with the Unemployment Benefit Officer. He may be entitled to some form of Supplementary Benefit. He should take with him copies of recent bills, eg heating, lighting, mortgage, etc.

7. If supplementary benefit is not available, the person may still qualify for rent rebate, rates rebate or a rent allowance. To claim any of these benefits, the appropriate application form should be obtained from the local Treasurer's or Housing Departments.

8. If a bank account is held, the whole financial situation should be discussed with the bank manager. Any building society or hire purchase company with which an account is held should be notified as soon as possible.

9. As the picture unfolds, there will be an inevitable tendency to become depressed and worried about the prospect of being unemployed and how to cope with the financial pressures. It is imperative that at this time, the momentum of 'things to be done' should be maintained.

10. Perhaps the most helpful way of presenting this programme to both husband and wife is as follows:
  a. Analyse all unnecessary expenditure, and take instant action to alleviate the immediate financial pressure.

b. Think of the finding of a new job as in itself a full-time job. In other words, spend the hours of the working day actively pursuing employment.

c. Resist the temptation to find out how the old firm is doing and what the old colleagues are up to. It can be an exercise in self-pity or masochism, and it only serves to look backwards and generate bitterness and resentment. This should be a time of looking forward, to the new opportunities that might arise out of the situation.

11. To begin with, this period of full-time job-hunting should be used as a time for reviewing what should now be the direction and purpose of life. In career terms, this might mean:

a. Immediate job-hunting.

b. Learning a new skill.

c. Using the time to start a small business or to enter into self-employment.

d. Furthering one's education.

Similarly, in terms of the family, the job-hunter ought to consider how to use the time together in the best way. This might mean:

a. Taking the children to school, sharing in their play and bed time.

b. Working out a joint routine that is compatible with seeking fulfilment of career ambitions.

c. Taking time out to talk to each other, maybe even go for walks; but above all confront the problems together and air misgivings as they arise.

d. Recognise that reduced income is going to lead to a change in social habits, and discuss how that time and energy can be best utilised.

12. To help in this 'stock-taking', get the person to draw up a list of answers to the following questions, and then to place them in order of priority.

a. How much time should I devote to family? to paid employment? to church? to recreation?

b. What sphere of creative work do I most enjoy? Could I earn my living from it?

c. How well do I fit into an employee environment?

d. Do I have the energy and ability to be self-employed?

e. What is the minimum that I and my family can afford to live on?

f. What occupations have given me most satisfaction?

g. What negative effect has work had on my private life?

h. What negative effects has my private life had on my work?

i. Are there any health considerations?

j. What has created the most pressure in my life?

k. What activities excite and motivate me?

l. What skills and talents do I have?

In answering these questions and putting them into an order of priority, a picture will emerge. Available options will become clear, ranging from the ideal to the totally unacceptable. This can lead a person to rethink the part that paid employment should play in the context of his life as a whole. Frequently people who have carried out this exercise have been able to turn talents which were being used only part-time into full-time self-employment.

This exercise also gives the unemployed person a real understanding not just of what he or she might want to do, but also why. This is very important, because it offers the individual a sense of purpose, and at the same time it can be helpful in preparing to explain to a prospective employer why one thinks one may be suitable for a job, or to a bank manager why he should lend the bank's money to start a new venture.

13. If, as a result of this analysis, the most effective solution seems to be to get a job as an employee, there are certain practical things that need to be done.

a. Write a curriculum vitae and get it typed. It should include:

Personal details – name, address, telephone number, date of birth, marital status, age of children.

Education – schools, qualifications, and any courses attended, with dates.

Hobbies and interests

Additional information – such as car driver/owner, clean driving licence, languages if appropriate, pre-paredness to relocate.

Career history – name of company, dates of employment, nature of business, job title, job responsibility, any achievements in the job worthy of note, why you left the job, finishing salary.

The job of the CV is to sell the applicant as a first-rate potential employee and secure an interview. When you have drafted the CV with the unemployed person, show it to another independent person. Set up a 'role play' of the interview, in which you or somebody else probes what an interviewer might consider weak points.

b. The person you are counselling should be constantly reminded that getting a job is a highly competitive occupation in its own right. Urge him to consider all avenues for marketing himself, and to try them all at once rather than one at a time. Interesting advertisements should be answered, the Job Centre or PER (Professional Executive Register) should be investigated, and the person should register with every employment agency likely to cover his skills. A list of local companies can be obtained from the library, town hall or local Chamber of Commerce. These should be circulated, asking for the details to be kept on file if no current openings exist.

The newspapers should be scanned, the Local Development Officer approached, and building sites visited, all in an attempt to find out what companies may be moving into the area. Then the applicant should write direct to them at their present address before they move, so that he is first in line for any jobs that might result from the move.

The covering letter should be typed and checked over by a third party before sending it. Each application should be considered individually, and an attempt made to find out what the company does, and to relate the experience of the applicant to the firm. Only the most obviously suitable applicants are going to get the interview!

c. If the applicant succeeds in getting an interview, he or she may well need some help in preparing for it. The main considerations are really common sense. Care should be taken with appearance, adequate time allowed to get to the interview promptly, and the company researched in advance. Simple yes/no answers to questions should be avoided, and replies should be as full as possible so the interviewer can get a glimpse of the candidate's personality. He should be advised not to smoke at the interview, to be as polite as he knows how, to try to be confident without being big-headed. The interview should be rehearsed in advance.

Above all else, however many disappointments there have been before, each interview should be treated as a new challenge and approached with a determination to get the job.

14. If, on the other hand, analysis indicates that the best course of action is to try to become self-employed, then similarly there are many things to be done.

Many of the factors involved in starting a new business are discussed in other parts of this book, but a check list of initial actions is given here. They consist of determining

   a. The likely rise of the market for what is to be sold, whether it be goods or services.
   b. The sales price the market will bear.
   c. The gross profit the product or service will produce.
   d. The means of marketing – direct mail, advertising, selling by telephone or by personal visit.
   e. The unavoidable overheads.
   f. The likely profitability.
   g. The cashflow.

h. The staff needed to support the operation (if any).

i. The competition.

All these factors need a very detailed analysis, and will be required as part of any proposal to be put forward when requesting financial support. As these areas are investigated they will inevitably create more questions. In which areas will specialist help be needed – ie legal services, accountancy, marketing, sales, production, administration? A counsellor, or a counselling centre, is likely to have access to such help and will be able to refer appropriate persons to the specialists.

These are hurdles put up not to depress but to be overcome. Considerable help does exist for the potential entrepreneur. For example,

The Enterprise Allowance Scheme (MSC).

The Small Firms Service – a service by the Department of Trade and Industry.

Training for Enterprise – a series of MSC courses.

The National Co-operative Development Agency, for promoting and advising on co-operative ventures.

Livewire – to encourage and support those between 16 and 25.

The Development Commission, for rural businesses.

Headstart – helping 17- to 22-year-olds to get going with their own enterprises.

Youth Businesses Initiatives – to help the under-25s in starting new businesses.

Project Fullemploy – self-employment training courses.

(Details of these organisations are given at the end of this book.)

Similarly there is a considerable range of written material available to give greater in-depth assistance and advice to the person considering setting up his or her own enterprise.

As can be seen, the whole area of pastoral care and counselling the unemployed is a critical and much-needed service, but is also one which needs considerable technical skills. The individual can give a great deal of help –

particularly if he or she has management or other business experience – but there are often cases where the counselling experience and gifts of a team can be more helpful.

Examples of 'drop in' counselling centres

Two examples of Community Projects, both providing pastoral outreach to the unemployed community, are given below.

The Cedarwood Centre

The Cedarwood Centre is based on a housing estate in North Shields. It serves a population of approximately 1,000 people, of which 46% are one-parent families and about 85% are unemployed.

When the local authority failed to establish a 24-hour child care centre on the estate, the North Tyneside Social Services and the Newcastle Diocesan Board of Social Responsibility took over the premises.

The Centre comprises four inter-connected, minimally adapted council houses. The staffing is primarily paid for by the diocese.

Hospitality is provided for local residents for 12 hours a day, Monday to Saturday. Facilities are provided for launderette, kitchen, pay-phone, television, typewriter, duplicator and sewing machines.

A Church Action on Poverty group meets on the estate, and contacts have begun to be made with wealthier groups with a view to understanding the real problems of the community on the estate.

David Peel, the organiser of the Centre, told me:

> The problems of really low self-worth are truly evident here. It is the biblical concept of those inside the city wall who are safe and warm, and those outside the wall who are the rejects. One young girl summed up the way many feel when she said, 'Of course, you don't realise – we're rubbish.'

In his Gospel, Mark tells us of one person who was outside the city wall: Legion, the demoniac. Jesus cared for him, and healed him, and when he had done so he commanded the man to 'tell them what the Lord has done for you'. The man went off, and spread the news in all the Ten Towns of what Jesus had done for him; and 'they were all amazed'.

Whole sections of our society are living 'outside the city wall'. Their self-estimate is 'We're rubbish'. Yet Jesus teaches us that by the power of the Holy Spirit they not only can be healed, but will also spread the Good News.

In the midst of this whole situation we are continually reminded of the true value of mankind in the sight of God and the calling we have to heal the sick, the depressed, the mentally wounded and those who feel that they live 'outside the city wall'.

The Cedarwood Centre is, in the words of David Peel, 'flat broke – penniless'; and there are many other similar organisations around the country.

St Matthew's Bestwood

On Nottingham's Bestwood Estate, the Church of St Matthew has opened its doors to provide a centre offering practical help, welfare rights advice, and legal advice. A Good Neighbour scheme is under way, and a self-help group for unemployed people. The estate is a council estate with 8,000 residents, more than 30% of whom are unemployed.

If your church does not live in this kind of community, then it is always possible to help an existing centre financially. On the other hand, if this kind of need is near at hand, then look to your church's resources and see what projects *you* can undertake 'to open the gates of the inner city'.

Other schemes exist which offer exactly this service. The Exmouth Enterprise Association, operating out of the basement of a Methodist church, is one that provides a counselling service. Balham and Tooting Youth Outreach Centre; Green Action Project in Houghton Green, Greater Manchester; The Cygnet Centre in Selby, North Yorkshire;

Crawley Centre for the Unemployed; Idle Baptist Church Advice Centre in Bradford, and 'Becenta' Community Enterprise in Luton, are all Christian action groups involved in this service, and are practical examples of ways in which Christians can help, and make their faith relevant to, a contemporary dilemma. The problem is that there are all too few of them, and there needs to be a conscious soul-searching by churches to consider whether by dint of their own efforts they can expand the current services.

Job Exports

'Lateral thinking' is a fashionable concept these days. It was popularised by Edward de Bono, who devised ingenious puzzles, the solution of which depended on completely abandoning all the conventional ways of looking at the problem and attempting to find a radically new way. The benefit of lateral thinking in a number of business and industrial environments has been that solutions which appeared to be unorthodox, and quite wrong by conventional standards, in fact often did the job and achieved results faster and more efficiently than the 'normal' techniques.

In dealing with unemployment, the unconventional approach often pays dividends. A situation in business that has always been solved a particular way can often yield benefits both to the business and to local unemployed, if a new way of doing things can be worked out. An example of this kind of thinking follows.

Remember – in dealing with unemployment, it pays to think sideways!

The import factor

The large number of imported goods in the shops, and the apparently increasing share of the home consumer market that those imports represent, is often one of the most difficult factors for somebody who is unemployed to come to terms with. It's natural to think that if we could only impose stringent import barriers the problem of unemployment would be solved. After all, domestic demand would remain the same; but instead of that demand being met by overseas labour in the shape of imported goods, the tariff barriers would price imported goods out of the market. Demand would be satisfied by UK products – which, by definition, means UK labour and UK jobs.

It's an attractive prospect, but sadly, not supported by reality.

What are the facts? Firstly, the United Kingdom is simply not self-sufficient in raw material and food, so it has to export manufactured goods in order to create the wealth with which these essential products can be imported from abroad. Secondly, in order to achieve this our products must be as competitive in price, quality, reliability, servicing and delivery as are those of our overseas competitors. It follows inevitably that in Britain survival means high productivity, good design, good marketing and effective management.

If import tariffs were to be imposed, the result would be that British consumers would either be forced to buy the (higher priced) British products or would be forced to pay even more for the imported products plus the tariff they carried. The result would be that the cost of living in the United Kingdom would rise, and that everybody would have less money available to spend on the British goods that really are competitive.

To add to that, any imposition of tariffs by Britain would certainly mean that there would be retaliatory action by our traditional overseas trading partners (just as we would be forced to retaliate if they imposed tariffs on our exports). And that might well mean that British goods which have hitherto proved competitive overseas would be much less marketable. It works both ways!

Any reduction in demand for British goods overseas would lead, of course, to further job losses. Also, we are members of a commom market – the European Economic Community – and that implies free trade between its members.

There is no short cut to survival. The nation's economy must be highly productive and innovative, or it will not survive at all.

The thrust of this section is not, therefore, to explore methods of avoiding realities which are in fact inescapable; but rather to look much more closely at those parts of the British economy where jobs are being exported by default, to see whether a lateral solution exists.

Export by inertia

The first aspect of job exports to be considered are those exports where the capacity and ability to produce a competitive product exists in the UK, but production does not happen due to a lack of information and awareness.

The reason often lies at an early stage of the production process. When a product is first designed, buyers and designers draw up the necessary engineering specifications for the components that will be required. These are then given part numbers and descriptions. It is often the case – unless something goes seriously wrong with quality, delivery or price – that the supplier, once found, is not later changed.

What this can mean is that if a UK supplier cannot be found at the beginning of the product development cycle, the supplier will turn out to be a foreign supplier either operating direct or (more usually) through a UK agent. It can be extremely difficult to make a case later for the supplier to be changed so that a UK firm can benefit.

Often in running businesses in the UK, I have found products being imported that could easily be produced in Britain with just the same or better quality, delivery and price; not least because the UK product does not have to carry the high costs of importation.

Channels of communication

With a large percentage of our society looking for opportunities to work, I am convinced that we should be creating a forum of discussion between manufacturers and job creators, whereby this kind of information can be distributed and the resources of local manufacturers examined. It could even be in the manufacturers' interest to give substantial help to such a project. The benefits to them might include local supply, goodwill from the local community, and at the same time a shortening of the channels of communication and supply.

During the war there were hardly any opportunities to import goods, and companies found themselves heavily dependent on domestic supply. All over Britain companies had cottage industries supplying them, and in many cases these small industries were set up by the purchasing companies themselves.

What is lacking at present is the know-how, the will and the imagination which are all necessary to establish the channels of communication in the first place. Most company directors appear to take the view that it is up to the entrepreneur to first produce his product and then present it to the buyer; the appraisal of the entrepreneur's quality is often made according to his ability to conform to this pattern. But often the problem is that an unemployed individual has the ability, the guts and the will to have a go at being self-employed; but he or she simply does not know what to produce, or, indeed what the market wants.

The costs of conducting such research might turn out to be a profitable investment for an employer, despite the fact that it would be an additional short-term burden at a time when all businesses are under some degree of financial pressure. The results could be exciting, and involve increased employment, a more competitive end product, and an improvement in the national balance of trade figures.

Local opportunities in retail trouble-shooting

In retailing it is a common practice to pay for imported goods by pre-paid letter of credit. On arrival they are inspected by a qualified goods-in quality controller.

If the goods do not meet the buyer's criteria, then the scenario frequently follows this pattern; they are rejected, and telex messages, telephone messages and the like result in the product being shipped back, for replacement. However, in the case of most faults in this type of situation, the goods are in fact received back by the original manufacturer who then repairs the fault and re-exports back to the customer.

The priorities of the two parties in this situation are clear enough. The *retailer* wants to be sure:

1. That he is receiving good-quality products for his customers;

2. That they are available when his customer needs them; and

3. That the transaction is turned over as quickly as possible, providing a fair return on the capital employed.

The priorities of the *overseas manufacturer* are that he wants to be sure:

1. That he will be able to satisfy *his* customer, the retailer.

2. That his goods will be turned around as quickly as possible.

3. That the products will be put right at the least possible cost.

Given these priorities, it is possible that the interests of both parties may best be served by not sending the products back overseas at all (the 'conventional' solution), but by allowing the faults to be put right by a local labour force (the lateral approach). In that way the retailer's quality is assured, the products will be available more quickly, and the investment in the purchase of the products is turned over more quickly. Similarly, the manufacturer knows that his customer's needs are satisfied more quickly without the associated costs of trans-shipment.

Two companies that have used these methods successfully are Tesco (Home 'n' Wear division) in Milton Keynes, and MFI in Northampton, both of whom have used them in their central warehouses with excellent – and profitable – results.

The significant benefit to the community is that though the

work is intermittent, it can provide additional real employment.

These are just two examples drawn from my own experience of working in industry. There are certainly many more. What I am proposing is not to subsidise jobs at the expense of fair competition, but to stimulate employers and employees alike to realise that the decisions they are taking – usually because they have always taken such decisions in the past – may be having implications for local job creation.

There is such a great need for genuine job creation that these questions need to be asked of local employers, and by local employers. Also, there is a need for an intermediary body which will bring together local businesses and individuals prepared to set up in business.

If Christians and the Church are to be effective in challenging the unemployment problem, then questioning the way companies are operating, and talking to local employers, must form part of their initiative for action.

It could well be that in some circumstances the dialogue will not only result in more real jobs, but also in increased efficiency and excellent local public relations for the companies concerned.

Co-operatives

We have so far talked about several aspects of new businesses and entrepreneurism as a way of helping the unemployed. But for many people it can be a frightening experience to start a business on one's own. There are so many factors – not only the responsibilities that will be involved, but also the prospect of being entirely on one's own and the fear of what lies ahead.

When the unknown affects oneself, it is bad enough. Whatever form the new business takes, it will mean leaving either the security of an existing work structure where ultimate responsibility does not rest on one's own shoulders, or the relative security of unemployment benefit where money arrives at known intervals and in known, if small, quantities.

But when the unknowns affect other people, who will be employed in the new enterprise and will need salaries, office facilities and reasonable working conditions, the fears of the potential entrepreneur can escalate to such a level that the new enterprise may never get off the ground.

This is one reason for the fact that one of the fastest-growing areas of successful new businesses is that of worker co-operatives. There are other reasons too, of course. In many cases businesses are being created that could not be operated as 'sole trader' enterprises. In a co-operative, resources are multiplied in terms of funding, talents and manpower.

A co-operative is, as its name implies, a business run by its workers. It is only genuine if it is controlled equally by all the working members. A co-operative must be registered either under the Industrial Common Ownership Movement rules, or under rules approved by the Register of Friendly Societies.

Throughout Europe, some 14,000 co-operatives exist which are genuinely worker-owned, employing over half a million people.[6] In the United Kingdom, many enterprise agencies have been started to help stimulate this sector of the job market, and already over 1,000 such ventures exist.

Finding out more

If you want to find out more about how a co-operative works, the starting point is the Co-operative Development Agency. This was set up in 1978 by Parliament with all-party support, to promote the co-operative sector in England and Northern Ireland. The equivalent agency in Wales is the Wales Co-operative Centre, and in Scotland, the Scottish Co-operative Development Committee.

The agency can give general guidance and assistance to potential co-operative businesses, but does not have funds of its own to invest.

The advantages of co-operatives

The chief advantages are as follows:

1. There is a built-in stimulus to be successful, because all the employees own and control a part of the business.

2. Current legislation gives a co-operative many of the advantages of a partnership, together with those of a limited liability company.

3. Decisions are shared and discussed between people, all of whom have a financial stake and involvement in what they are discussing.

4. The responsibilities are shared – and so are the rewards.

Industrial Common Ownership Finance Limited

One of the most impressive recommendations for co-operative enterprise is in the record of Industrial Common Ownership Finance Limited (ICOF).

This organisation grew out of the Industrial Common Ownership Movement in 1974, and has developed excellent organisational skills in assessing co-operative investment and has achieved an excellent financial record in this area.

The organisation operates with a board of ten elected Directors known as 'Trustees'. The board meets quarterly to discuss and consider policy issues such as rates of interest, methods of lending, monitoring procedures and financial reports. The Advances and Monitoring Sub-committee meets monthly to consider new loan applications and receive reports on monitoring visits made to borrowers. Loans over £10,000 are referred to the Trustees for confirmation.

The procedures for applying for a loan are similar to those required by a bank. A formal application is made, together with a supporting business prospectus which contains information on business plans and financial projections. Help is given by ICOF officers who visit the co-operative on site and advise on how best to prepare the application.

Most loans average between £5,000 and £15,000 and capital repayments are typically spread over a period of about five years. The monthly repayments usually commence only six months after the loan has been made.

Day-to-day business is dealt with by a small professional staff of four.

Since its inception, ICOF has lent £520,000 to 51 new co-operative enterprises, covering almost every business one can imagine. As at January 1983, £295,020 was on loan to 30 co-operatives employing 320 people. Since 1974, loans to the level of £120,000 have been repaid and reloaned. Throughout its history, only 15% of ICOF funds have had to be written off, which is a considerably better track record than, for example, the government guarantee loan scheme to new businesses can claim.

Not all ICOF loans are made to new businesses starting up. Some cover recoveries of businesses which are being re-established on a co-operative basis; such as the frequent cases reported in the media where a business with crippling financial problems is sold to its workers for a nominal sum. The workers acquire control but are immediately faced with all the liabilities and outgoings of the company. In similar circumstances, ICOF has made loans.

Loans are also made for the purpose of expanding existing co-operatives.

The ICOF lends only to co-operatives in the West Midlands, but it provides a marvellous practical example for other organisations considering similar endeavours.

The Industrial Common Ownership Movement

ICOM is the other important organisation working in the field of co-operatives.

This is a national support organisation, and some 95% of all new co-operatives are helped by it. It is able to consult and give advice on the problems of starting up as well as often providing free legal, accountancy or marketing help.

Church involvement

Many churches will be interested in examining co-operatives with a view to support, either by contributing financially to the success of an existing enterprise, or by helping in the creation of a new co-operative which might be composed of Christians, or those who are not Christians, or both.

There are now some 80 local co-operative development agencies, all of whom are geared to helping people who are considering setting up a co-operative enterprise. These are obvious sources of information when advice is needed in the context of local conditions.

A church that is considering giving assistance to a job creation programme may well, in view of reports of the funding success of ICOF, consider the co-operative route as well worth investigating. One straightforward way of getting involved is to contribute financially to an existing organisation such as ICOF.

Unfortunately, the possible ways of supporting ICOF are restricted, as under the terms of the Banking Acts the organisation is only allowed to receive grants or gifts. It cannot receive loans intended for on-lending to co-operatives. However, if a church wishes to commit itself financially to supporting this method of job creation, it is useful to know that ICOF can arrange 'marriages' between those looking for funding and those looking for co-operatives to which to lend.

In addition, ICOF is organised to give advice and information to any local agency or local authority that wishes to establish an independent fund – help which includes setting up full administrative procedures.

So, if you decide to commit your resources in this direction, help is available.

I believe that the future of the co-operative movement is promising.

In addition, it can be argued that it is scripturally well-based. Since money is only one of the many ingredients required to make a successful business, it seems that there is something inherently wrong with a situation in which an 'absentee landlord' can dictate the future of people's jobs and careers, when his only contribution to the business is his money.

It is a situation that can be all too often abused. To expect employees to be happy when they are continually worried about whether or not they will have a job tomorrow creates a very difficult environment. Similarly, to be in the position of having no say in the future of a company or its practices and policies can lead to considerable strains and, not infrequently, problems of dual standards.

That does not mean that there is no such thing as a badly run co-operative, nor that there are no sole traders or limited companies that are well organised, ethically based, and with good communications between employees and management.

However, in a co-operative the power given to the individuals who have contributed the money is considerably diluted, the various contributions of other members are properly recognised, and all members have the chance to participate in policy decisions.

Co-operatives have a legitimate and growing role in the world of employment, and should be given thorough consideration as a candidate for church support.

The early retirement debate

Rightly, in view of the shocking statistics, the plight of the unemployed young people is often in the news and makes the biggest headlines. But, as we have already seen, there is considerable hardship at the other end of the age scale, where large numbers of older people are also unemployed.

In March 1978 *The Department of Employment Gazette* published estimates made by the Department of the cost of bringing forward the official male retirement age from 65 to 60 years, to bring them into line with women.

At that time the effect would have been to reduce registered unemployment by nearly 200,000 in the first year of the scheme's operation, building up to 600,000 as the numbers of those approaching retirement age increased. The net cost to the Exchequer, at 1978 prices, would have been in the order of just over £1,000 million.

On these figures, early retirement would be far more cost-effective in generating employment than any other scheme currently being pursued.

The social benefits of such a scheme are very considerable. Male life expectancy at age 60 is only 14.8 years. Female employment – with a statutory retirement age of 60 – is increasing. If the male retirement age were lowered to match that of the female, married couples in which both partners survived to 60 could look forward to a longer period of life together after retirement.

For many in that situation the need to work would still exist – though not necessarily in a paid job – and for many people such a scheme would not be at all suitable. At the very least, a new problem would be created in terms of devising adequate pre-retirement courses and in making sure that those taking advantage of early retirement retained a real sense of being needed and valuable members of the community.

Perhaps this is an area in which there would be an increased role for the churches in making use of the experience and interpersonal skills of the older person in pastoral work in the community, and also in providing work projects designed not to patronise the retired elderly but to enable them to contribute in a meaningful and satisfying way to the general health of the community.

Already many companies are contemplating early retirement schemes, and some have already made it part of company policy to implement them. But for the majority of firms the matter is not even given consideration, let alone properly investigated or discussed with the work force.

It goes without saying that the whole issue calls for considerable sensitivity, especially when first proposed. But if a well-considered programme of discussion with those likely to be affected were to be conducted, it could lead to the creation of many thousands of jobs for young unemployed people.

An Action in Retirement Centre

The members of Bishopswearmouth Parish Church were really concerned at the way in which Sunderland inner city development was affecting the life of the church, so they appointed someone to develop a town centre ministry. At the same time Age Concern were looking for ways of providing positive help for the large numbers of people in the area who, at the age of 50-plus, had been made redundant.

A proposal was put to the PCC that they should undertake, with aid and grant assistance, to fund the conversion of part of the church buildings into an Action in Retirement Centre. With dwindling congregations, the buildings were not being used to anything like their full capacity, especially during the week. The PCC accepted the suggestion, and with fund-raising, Urban Aid grants and private grants, between 1978 and 1981 one third of the parish church was converted into a Centre.

The job was done, with considerable skill, by a church architect. Even though the restaurant is in the church it in no way detracts from its function as an amenity nor its function as a place of worship.

The organisation operates in the following main areas:

1. Counselling those who have been made redundant, are coming up to retirement, or have just retired. Most of the counselling takes place in the home, so that other members of the family can be involved if appropriate. Sometimes requests are made to meet on neutral ground, in a cafe or pub. Occasionally the meetings take place at the centre. 'We are really involved in grief counselling,' said Marjorie Bird, organiser. 'It is as if someone had been bereaved, and the shock and depression follow a very similar pattern.'

2. A job bureau exists to help find alternative work, but in Sunderland it is a desperately hard struggle.

3. Accepting therefore that prospects of paid employment for this age group are slender, the Centre sets out to occupy people both physically and mentally so that the work involvement is replaced by other creative outlets. Realising that the need for creative work and expression lasts throughout life, they have provided a huge range of activities. The organisation has managed to obtain the use of the local Polytechnic pool for an hour each morning, and recently an 89-year-old completed a beginners' swimming course.

There are keep-fit classes, embroidery, lessons in local history, beginners' French, Spanish, German and now an advanced French course. Music appreciation, two ramblers' groups (designed to suit the stamina), ballroom dancing, and self-defence are all activities that thrive.

An additional building has opened nearby which has been fitted out largely by unemployed members who are craftsmen, to suit the needs of the Centre for amenities for other art and craft skills – such as photography, painting, pottery and woodwork.

It is in this activity that Marjorie Bird sees the opportunity for unemployed people to teach their craft skills to others, and so generate a form of self-help group.

The church continues to be involved in the Centre, and has many members who regularly attend. Three PCC members sit on the management committee. There are Bible Study classes, and a Christian Forum held regularly to provide an opportunity for teaching, witness and discussion.

Marjorie Bird comments:

> Most of the people come to us psychologically shattered, but through the expertise of counselling and keeping people mentally and physically busy, we help them to come to grips with their job loss and try to create a new, worthwhile way of life.
>
> Our people are, in the main, young old people who have found other ways of helping and giving to society by channelling their creative abilities into other areas than paid work.

The Centre offers expertise to other organisations and firms, offering advice and help on planning pre-retirement courses to help those facing retirement to think more positively about the prospect. It also provides courses for professionals working with older people.

Each week, at the height of the activities, some 1,500 people visit or participate in activities at the Centre.

Despite all the good work being done here, the Centre is

continually in need of financial help. Says Marjorie Bird,

> The operation is run on a shoestring, and we always seem to have the begging bowl out. Fundraising efforts such as jumble sales and the like just keep the wolf from the door. We desperately need more help. The problems with which we deal are growing, not diminishing. We need people to visit, and identify with what we are trying to do. We need their prayers as well as their money.
>
> The uncertainty that relates to MSC support for some of the workers' wages (since they are only on 52-week contracts), together with the problems of the huge turnover of staff this gives, and problems of continuity, all add to the organisational problems. The previous organiser managed to get a one-year extension to his contract, but this is unusual and is the absolute limit to the MSC scheme.
>
> We feel that we are really meeting an important need here, and would welcome other groups from around the country visiting us, and/or getting advice on how to set up their own scheme.

It is a challenge. How does what is happening in Sunderland relate to your own locality?

Church twinning

As we examine the statistics of unemployment, one factor stands out above all the others. Where there is most unemployment – notably in the north of England – the Church, almost by definition, has fewest resources, particularly financial, to meet the needs. By the same definition, churches in the south where the problems are generally speaking much less severe, often have the resources with which something really worthwhile could be done. In the areas of high unemployment, where I have talked to members of churches undertaking real action programmes – particularly those involving themselves in new business start-up – lack of resources and particularly lack of finance is a constant handicap.

Is there some way in which the assets of the wealthy south can be used to help the fight against unemployment in the north? It is a question that has concerned many who have grappled with social problems.

Many churches, through their departments of social responsibility where such exist, have diverted some church funds to assist churches elsewhere that can demonstrate that they have worthwhile projects and needs.

However, many denominations do not have such machinery, and the concept of funds going through a faceless clearing house lacks much of the immediacy that is perhaps necessary to stimulate the right response from a congregation. It is much easier to establish a commitment to a situation that one knows and keeps up to date with, than to an organisation that exists simply to hand on money.

We would like to propose, as one method of establishing that commitment, that churches consider developing what might be called 'church twinning'. Just as the overseas aid organisations have found it helpful to encourage people who contribute money to identify with where that money is going and what it will be used for, so similar benefits would come from church twinning.

What we are proposing is a direct commitment between the Christians of one church who are seeking an opportunity to obey the biblical command to share what they have, and a church in an area of high unemployment which has projects for which it needs financial support.

Ideally, what is needed is an organisation that can put the two in touch with each other. As such an organisation does not exist at present, churches with needs should consider appealing through church magazines and newspapers for help; and churches willing to give help should similarly advertise their presence.

When the two have made contact there should be a series of meetings between interested members of both churches, alternating between churches. Realistic assessments of needs and resources should be undertaken. Of course, any long-term commitment that is entered into ought if possible to receive any statutory aid or rebates available – for example, every tax-paying church member should be aware of the advantages of covenanting gifts.

If the scheme is to continue for a meaningful period of time there needs to be a spiritual as well as a financial link. We envisage a very special kind of relationship developing between the twinned churches. They might exchange prayer letters, occasionally exchange pulpits, keep each other well informed of their activities, encourage inter-church visits and become closer and closer in many ways.

It would be absolutely imperative that church twinning should not be entered into if either party thinks of it as charity. It is not, and every effort should be made to prevent such an attitude developing. Funds should be made available not to the individuals concerned but to the agency that the receiving church is using to organise the financial structuring of projects. Anything smacking of 'thank you letters' should be studiously spurned.

Perhaps a good analogy is the co-operative, where the member putting up the money has no greater status in the organisation than the member who organises the truck rotas. Twinned churches are in a co-operative, and the excitement of the challenge is that it will often be a co-operative that spans the nation.

Church Action with the Unemployed (CAWTU) will act as a broker between churches and, with its current ecumenical and geographical structure, is well placed to introduce one church to another. CAWTU details are given at the end of this book.

Church twinning is quite simply the pooling of resources, both material and spiritual, in order to tackle a problem neither can solve on their own, and to bear witness to the God who grieves over his fallen world.

Part 4: How to Get Organised

We hope very much that you have read this book with a growing conviction that you would like to do something to help in the unemployment crisis, and that you would like to give that help in the context of Church involvement.

If that is so, then in all probability the question that is uppermost in your mind now is: exactly how do you get things started?

You probably do not have all the skills and abilities needed to do the things you would like to do on your own – nobody can embark on a project like this without help and support. But neither can you just pass the book on to your minister or a local businessman (and in any case, by the same token, they could not do anything on their own either!). Action of the kind we are talking about must result from a group of people who are willing to set aside time, talents and resources to pray together, to work together, and to help each other.

The key to mobilising such a group is organisation. If your church is to be a really effective force in the fight against unemployment, then, as in any undertaking, there must be plan and priorities. The vast majority of Christians, at the level of the emotions, are deeply concerned about all the issues that are raised in this book. This is genuine compassion, and the tears are real. Nevertheless, if a church does not organise itself efficiently, all the concern in the world will do little to change the situation.

So – how *do* you get started?

To start with, a meeting should be called of all church members. The particular impetus for this meeting might be any of a number of factors; a desire to do something for the unemployed in the church and/or in the neighbourhood, perhaps, or a period of intense interest in the subject by the media, or just a significant number of church members individually having a burden for the unemployed and bringing it to the church as a matter of urgent discussion.

The meeting should seek to discuss the national and local

situation in the light of the Bible. Every effort should be made to avoid letting the meeting become a battleground of opinions, and the members should be encouraged to look beyond their local knowledge to view the national situation as well. You may like to use some of the figures presented in this book to prepare a factsheet which can be given to every member.

The purpose of the meeting should be to reach agreement that the problem is one of home mission which requires urgent involvement by the church.

As a first step towards that involvement a church member should be elected to make a detailed study of the local unemployment situation, and to report back to a further meeting. If you are the person who has organised the meeting you may well find yourself landed with the task! But it is an absolutely essential stage and must be undertaken.

At the same time there needs to be agreement that the national problem will be the subject of consistent prayer in the church's various prayer and fellowship meetings. No work of God can survive without a backing of sustained prayer. I have been struck by the number of people working in this field who say that without people praying for the project, it could not continue.

Getting the facts

The person who has been appointed to prepare the initial report then needs to embark on the following programme of research.

1. Make contact with all the local churches, to establish whether they have a person appointed to a similar role, with whom you can share ideas. Establish whether any of the churches have already undertaken any projects in this area, or have plans under way to do so. Where the subject has not even been discussed, it may be that the contact will stimulate interest or provide an opportunity for the other church to join in the study.

Since in the end what will determine the projects that can be undertaken, and to what degree, will be the resources of time, talents and money, the wider the net can be spread to bring in additional help the better. Also, it is always very important in work of this nature that projects are well co-ordinated to avoid wasteful duplication.

Historically churches have frequently found considerable blessings in working together for common objectives, especially when wishing to witness to the community by some practical example of living out Christian discipleship. Such operations as the Fish Schemes, and other community care or self-help projects, have served not only to provide a valuable social service but have simultaneously brought Christians together in a working fellowship. This inevitably leads to better understanding and co-operation between churches which may not in the past have shared very much. Christian action on unemployment provides a similar stimulus for co-operation.

2. Contact the local Job Centre manager to discuss the level and nature of the problem locally. How many people are unemployed in the locality? What is the breakdown of age ranges, skills, length of time out of work, number of vacancies, type of vacancies, vacancies unfilled, skills required by local employers as opposed to skills available?

3. Contact the employment division of the Manpower Services Commission dealing with the Community Programme. This might be a Community Programme Link Team, or alternatively one of the many Community Programme managing agents, who can undertake to work for organisations that want to help but feel that they cannot initially sponsor their own schemes. The advantage of talking to one of the national agencies, which have major contracts with the MSC for a large number of Community Programme funded schemes, is threefold:

   a. They already have experience of mounting projects.
   b. They have the experience and administrative systems to ensure that a scheme would be effective, efficient and well managed.

c. They can also be a means of getting ideas and projects implemented quickly.

4. The same MSC offices should be able to provide details of the Voluntary Projects Programme. Like the Community Programme, this scheme works through project sponsors which can be any organisation or group of individuals. Its prime purpose is to help develop existing skills of the unemployed with a variety of voluntary jobs.

The programme can also help with the unemployed person's use of time, and sometimes acts as a helpful reintroduction to work for those who have been unemployed for a long period. Since the jobs are voluntary and officially recognised by the MSC as being part of the VPP, unemployed people can take part in the scheme while not affecting their right to statutory benefits.

Further information on these schemes can be obtained from the Volunteer Centre, or in Scotland from the Scottish Council for Social Service, or in Wales from the Council for Voluntary Action.

There are also Councils for Voluntary Service, Rural Community Councils and Volunteer Bureaux at local level which can provide more local information and advice.

5. Contact may well then be advisable with another group of people in the MSC, the Training Division, to discuss the various Youth Training Schemes, Information Technology Centres and Training Workshops.

6. Contact either the local person in authority or the local personnel manager of the major employers in the immediate vicinity to discuss employment needs, whether the local unemployed are lacking in education or training to suit those needs, what the future prospects for employment are, and whether the price of labour is inhibiting employment.

Ask how they might be able to help with management expertise or funds in involving themselves with a church project. Ask whether there are any temporary peaks in their business that might require additional temporary or seasonal labour. Ask whether products or components are having to be imported, which, with enterprise, could be manufactured locally.

7. Meet the local careers officers in the local schools to discuss future job prospects, education, training and any programmes that they have for assisting youngsters to acquire jobs.

8. Discuss with a few unemployed people the problems that they have had in obtaining work. How did they get interviews? How did they get on in the interview?

Ask how they spend their time.

9. Write to the National Council for Voluntary Organisations, which is primarily funded by the Home Office and whose function is to support both voluntary and community groups throughout the United Kingdom. The organisation advises on fund-raising and how to make contact with central and local government departments, gives information (and support) on community schemes and any locally based employment initiatives, and advises whether funding can be obtained through the European Social Fund.

The NCVO provides links with the Department of Environment Urban Programme, which is aiming to help economic regrowth, to improve the physical environment, and to organise local services to meet the needs of the local community. There are specially assisted areas under the Inner Cities Programme, which are designated 'Partnership and Programme Authorities'. Additional funds may be obtainable from the programme to help voluntary work projects.

Similarly, the NVCO can provide information on rural policy and explain how voluntary work initiatives can be helped in rural areas.

Forming an unemployment action group

When this research is completed, a report should be presented to the church showing the extent of the unemployment problem in the local area, what is already being done to assist in easing the problem and what response was obtained from local churches, employers and schools.

A committee should then be set up to assess the areas of greatest need. If your church is in a low unemployment area, discuss the possibility of church twinning and making contact with a church where the need is obviously greater, with a view to seeing how your church can help. However, if the report reveals considerable need, examine the suggestions contained in this book and study the feasibility of forming an unemployment action group and setting up similar operations. The committee should take an inventory of what time, talents and money exist in the church, and what proportion could be devoted to the unemployment action group.

Consideration should be given to work that the church members could generate in the following ways:

1. Jobs provided by church members in their homes.

2. Work that could be generated by members who are employers.

3. Money that could be raised to assist new business ventures.

4. An action programme with employers to discuss the relationship of the price of labour to employment.

5. An action programme with employers on work that could be generated by rethinking overtime policies.

6. An action programme with employers on early retirement policies.

7. An action programme with employers on job sharing.

8. An action programme with employers on work which may go abroad but which could be handled locally with new enterprise and initiative.

9. An action programme for a social centre to which unemployed people can go and discuss their problems.

10. An action programme for counselling; that is,

encouraging members to go on courses or otherwise receive professional instruction.

11. Discovering what management skills are available to the church to assist and advise new businesses and perhaps help ailing ones.

12. Considering what projects could be devised for a Community Programme scheme or Youth Training scheme.

13. Reviewing what facilities can be made available for training to improve job prospects.

14. Contacting Church Action with the Unemployed for help on church twinning, and making contact with another church with a view to giving or receiving help.

At all costs, great care must be taken to ensure that subsidy does not create a situation in which work is taken away from those already employed; though of course a self-financed, unsubsidised scheme can and should compete freely in the market.

For every project decided on, an individual with the necessary time and talents should be appointed to look after it and ensure its success. It is vitally important that you do not overstretch your resources. A scheme that starts up and folds after two months is simply playing with the needs of the unemployed.

Churches may even consider approaching the MSC with a view to appointing someone to head up operations on a full-time basis, funded through one of the MSC programmes.

Look closely at the situation of your own church. How much are the premises used? Many are used only on Sundays and weekday evenings. Perhaps you can free this resource, at least in part, for action on unemployment.

Many buildings could be adapted to provide excellent local social amenities; perhaps your group could discuss with the church the possibility of making its major contribution in the form of a conversion programme for the church premises.

Where renovation of church buildings has been postponed

or abandoned through lack of funds, finance to carry out the work, if the intention is to create a resource for a Community Programme Scheme or a Voluntary Projects Programme scheme, may be available through those organisations.

It goes without saying that these projects are in no way incompatible with – in fact are intrinsically part of – the Church's role as the visible, local community of God's people.

No matter what your situation is, there is *something* you can contribute. If you are a tiny church, join with others in the area. You may be the catalyst that gets the whole thing going. If your church is in an area with little immediate need, contact another church where the need is greater. If you are in an area where the needs are so great that your resources are inadequate, then call for help.

Make sure that the subject is discussed in practical ways, as well as (or instead of) theoretical ways, in Church synods and conferences. This will stimulate greater consideration as to how the churches can on a national scale marshal their resources to meet the needs.

You can always do *something*.

There is no excuse for doing nothing.

Conclusion: A Call to Action

The fundamental precept for any Christian is to live one's life to God's glory. In the Bible we find very simple teaching as to how his will should be expressed in our lives.

The Bible teaches us about God's perfect justice.

But where is the justice in people being denied the right to work, through no fault of their own? By what law of justice does lack of educational opportunity condemn somebody to years of joblessness? Where is the justice in people being denied the right to work because they happened to be born in one place rather than another? Or in people being prevented from providing for their families?

Christians are called to strive to ensure that God's will be done on earth, as it is in heaven.

So in setting out our priorities we should be giving first emphasis to the worst affected sectors of our society: ethnic minorities, single-parent families, areas of designated deprivation, and of course the under 25- and over 55-year-old age groups. All of these tend to be caught in the trap of long-term unemployment.

The Bible tells us also that work is not, in the eyes of God, the basis of human worth. As Paul reminds us in Ephesians 2, it is by grace we are saved, not through works. We need to hold this fundamental truth at the very heart of all our counselling and thinking, for it provides a context into which we ought to place the unemployment problem. Whilst it is, in our view, a deeply important thing to implement the proposals in this book, it is not the most important thing in life.

However, as we saw when we began this study, work was a basic creation ordinance. The Lord God took man and put him in the Garden of Eden to work it and take care of it, we read (Gen 2:15). In Genesis 1:28 we are told that God commanded man to be fruitful and to replenish and subdue the earth, and have dominion over every living thing upon the earth. Later this was embodied in the Ten Commandments (Exod 20:9): 'Six days shall you labour and do all your work.'

So to deny man the opportunity to work is to deny him the chance of fulfilling his very nature, and the basic laws by which God has ordained that man should live upon the earth.

The concept of how man should use his gift of dominion is later expressed in the numerous references to stewardship, which effectively makes man accountable to God for the use of all the world's resources. In our context, this includes the efficient and productive use of labour, as well as industrial and technological efficiency.

It is at this point that many theologians, politicians and economists break ranks and argue for whichever route, philosophy, or mathematical model appears to them to promise the correct balance for a just, obedient and well-ordered society; some include planned unemployment in their proposals.

But the fact remains that so far as the Christian in the pew is concerned, whatever the justification claimed for it, mass unemployment is a gross failure of our ability to exercise proper stewardship over the productive, creative, God-given resources of mankind.

In the book of Ecclesiastes there occurs a famous passage: 'There is a time for everything, and a season for every activity under heaven: a time to be born and a time to die . . .' (Eccles 3:1, 2). However, what is often forgotten is that the passage in due course comes to verse 13: 'That every man may eat and drink, and find satisfaction in all his toil – this is the gift of God.' The verse speaks of that healthy state in which every man has adequate means to live in dignity, and every job is one where the worker can find satisfaction in doing something useful and beneficial.

In today's world with all its material emphases, the equation that is often proposed is this: 'No job=no money=no life.' Though it is a wrong view of life it should be taken very seriously. When lack of money becomes such an anxiety that it preoccupies every waking hour, then the view becomes totally understandable.

Paul, writing to Timothy, put the problem into an absolute context.

But godliness with contentment is great gain. For

we brought nothing into the world, and we can take nothing out. But if we have food and clothing, we will be content with that. People who want to get rich fall into temptation and a trap and into many foolish desires that plunge men into ruin and destruction. For the love of money is a root of all kinds of evil. Some people, eager for money, have wandered from the faith and pierced themselves with many griefs. (1 Timothy 6:6–10)

He urges contentedness, without complacency; the need for life's necessities, and the danger of greed. It is a sobering statement of the simple value of having 'food and clothing'.

Such things are luxuries to the unemployed. There are few living on state benefit who can claim to be content because all their basic needs are met. Even were it not so, how should the rest of us be content, knowing that we enjoy so much more than the bare necessities – because we are fortunate enough to have work?

The Word of God lays a charge upon us. We must share our good fortune. We must care. Unemployment is a concern for the employed. The call to action is very clear.

Notes

Introduction

1. Michael Leroy, 'Liverpool 8 Update' *Third Way*, July–August 1984.

Part 1

1. William Beveridge, *'Full Employment in a Free Society'*, 1944.

Part 2

1. David Metcalf, 'On the Measurement of Employment and Unemployment' *National Institute Economic Review*, August 1984.
2. O.E.C.D., *Employment Outlook*, Tables 2, 3 and 4, September 1984.
3. Current *CoSIRA* Literature, reference BB2080.5.82.
4. R. Layard and S. Nickell, 'The Causes of British Unemployment' *National Institute Economic Review*, February 1985.
5. J. Northcott and P. Rogers, 'Microelectronics in British Industry – The Pattern of Change' *Policy Studies Institute*, March 1984.
6. *Department of Employment Gazette*, December 1982 and June 1983.
7. Department of Employment, 'Age and Duration Analysis of the Unemployed for Statistical date 11 April 1985', produced 16 May 1985.
8. *ibid*.
9. *ibid*.
10. National Council for Voluntary Organisations, 'Voluntary and Community Organisations and Long Term Unemployment' *An NCVO Consultation Paper*, March 1983.
11. Central Statistical Office, 'Employment Section' *Social Trends 15*, 1985 edition.
12. Central Statistical Office, 'Income and Wealth Section' *Social Trends 15*, Table 5.3, 1985 edition.
13. Patrick Minford, 'State Expenditure: a Study in Waste', Supplement to *Economic Affairs*, April–June 1984.

Part 3

1. The 282 Sections of the Laws of Hammurabi, King of Babylon circa 1792–1750 BC.
2. Obtainable from the Information Office, Department of Trade and Industry.

3. Business in the Community, 'Enterprise Agencies Section' *A Guide to Action* 1985.
4. Eduard Gaugler, 'Study on the effects of Job Sharing' 1981, cited in David Clutterbuck and Roy Hills, *The re-making of work*, published by Grant McIntyre and International Management.
5. Survey conducted in Spring 1981 by *International Management* and published in October 1981 issue.
6. *Action on Unemployment: 100 Projects with Unemployed People* (Church Action with the Unemployed, 1984).

CAWTU

Church Action with the Unemployed is the principal focal resource to enable all churches, of all denominations, to respond more effectively to the tragedy of unemployment.

If you are interested in Church Twinning, or wish to receive more information on what action other churches are taking, or need help, information, advice, publicity material or information about their Launchpad Direct Aid Grants, then write or telephone your local CAWTU contact.

Head Office:

146 Queen Victoria Street
London EC4V 4BY
Telephone (temporary) (076 389 272)

Local CAWTU Contacts

Bedford and Buckingham: The Rev'd David Everett, 43 Duncombe Street, Bletchley, Milton Keynes MK2 2LX (0908 648704)
Bexley: The Rev'd Antony Dalling, 30 Maiden Erlegh Avenue, Bexley, Kent DA5 3PD (0322 529776)
Birmingham: The Rev'd Denis Claringbull, Church House, Harborne Park Road, Birmingham B17 0BH (021 427 5141)
Black Country: The Rev'd Robin Blount, 9 Tansley Hill Road, Dudley, West Midlands DY2 7ER (0384 53084)
Bradford: Mr. David Waller, CRTU (Bradford), 1 Barker End Road, Bradford BD3 9AF (02741 308935)

Bristol and Swindon: The Rev's Louis Judson, Social and Industrial Ministry, The Cathedral, Bristol BS1 5TJ (0272 23944)

Cambridge: The Rev'd Ken Hawkings, 31 Thornton Close, Girton, Cambridge CB3 0NF (0223 276657)

Cheshire: The Rev'd Elliot Booth, Crew Green Vicarage, Crewe Green, Crewe CW1 1UN (0270 580118)

Corby: The Rev'd Canon Frank Scuffham, Stoke Albany Rectory, Market Harborough, Leicestershire LE16 8PZ (0858 85213)

Coventry: The Rev'd Trebor Cooper, Cathedral Offices, 7 Priory Row, Coventry CV1 5ES (0203 27597)

Croydon: The Rev'd David Curwen, 48 Northampton Road, Croydon CR0 7HT (01 654 4938)

Cumbria: The Rev'd Jim Hyslop, The Vicarage, Little Broughton, Cockermouth CA13 0YL (0900 825317)

Derbyshire: Miss Ann Morisy, Board for Social Responsibility, Church House, Full Street, Derby DE1 3DR (0332 382 233)

Devon: Mr. Martyn Goss, 96 Old Tiverton Road, Exeter EX4 6LD (0392 31366 or 78875)

Essex: c/o The Rev'd Canon Paul Brett, Council for Social Responsibility, 53 New Street, Chelmsford, Essex CM1 1NG (0245 58271)

Gloucestershire: The Rev'd Robert Naylor, The Rectory, Over Old Road, Hartpury, Gloucester GL19 3BJ (045 270 556)

Greater Manchester: The Rev'd Canon Alan Gawith, 27 Blackfriars Road, Manchester M3 7AQ (061 832 5253)

Grimsby: The Rev'd Canon John Rhodes, St. Luke's House, 17 Heneage Road, Grimsby DN32 9DZ (0472 43167)

Hartlepool: The Rev'd Michael Langford, St. James' Vicarage, Rossmere Way, Hartlepool, Cleveland (0429 73938)

Herts and Beds: Mr. Martyn Lloyd, 41 Holywell Hill, St. Albans AL1 1HE (0727 51748)

Hull: The Rev'd Michael Redfearn, 19 Bellfield Avenue, Hull HU8 9DS (0482 702033)

Lancashire: Mr. G. A. Jones, Haigton Cottage, Cow Hill, Grimsargh, Preston PR2 5SE (0772 653837)

Leeds: The Rev'd Canon Alan Griggs, 23 Harrowby Road, Leeds LS16 5HX (0532 758100 or 454268)

Leicester: The Secretary, Board for Social Responsibility, 278 East Park Road, Leicester LE5 5AY (0533 736535)

Lincoln: Mrs. Margaret Moon, Lincolnshire Churches Unemployment Resource Group, Swallowbeck Community Projects Agency, 509 Neward Road, Lincoln LN6 8TR (0522 40313)

Liverpool: The Rev'd Bob Dew, 26 Mather Avenue, Liverpool L18 5HS (051 724 1899)

London North: The Rev'd Francis Jakeman, 128 Pinner View, Harrow HA1 4RN (01 427 8678)
London South: The Rev'd Robert Nind, 27 Blackfriars Road, London SE1 8NY (01 733 8322 or 01 928 3970)
Maidstone and East Kent: The Rev'd Canon David Clift, 41 Buckland Hill, Maidstone, Kent ME16 0SA (0622 52062)
Norfolk: The Rev'd Canon John Room, 23 Cannons Close, Thetford, Norfolk (0842 2338)
Northampton: c/o The Rev'd Canon Frank Scuffham, Stoke Albany Rectory, Market Harborough, Leicestershire LE16 8PZ (0858 85213)
Nottingham: The Rev'd Eric Forshaw, 11 Clumber Crescent North, The Park, Nottingham NG7 1EY (0602 417156)
Peterborough: The Rev'd Mostyn Davies, 16 Swanspool, Peterborough PE3 7LS (0733 262034)
Teeside: The Rev'd John Wilcox, 21 Forth Road, Redcar, Cleveland TS10 1PN (0642 484393)
Salisbury and Poole (Dorset): The Rev'd Canon David Tizzard, Diocesan Office, Church House, Crane Street, Salisbury, Wiltshire SP1 2QB (0722 335876)
Scunthorpe: Mick Maskel, 100 Dale Street, Scunthorpe, South Humberside (0724 849159)
Selby: George Fairhurst, The Cygnet Centre, Union Lane, Selby, North Yorkshire YO8 0AU (0757 700131)
South Hampshire: Mr. Bill Markham, 1 Abbey Hill Road, Winchester, Hants SO23 7AT (0962 69248)
South Yorkshire: The Rev'd Michael Keen, 39 Tennyson Avenue, Mexborough, South Yorkshire S64 0AX (0709 583765)
Staffordshire: The Rev'd Geoffrey Babb, 9 Brunswick Terrace, Stafford ST16 1BB (0785 46838)
Suffolk: The Rev'd Geoffrey Cates, 13 Tower Street, Ipswich, Suffolk (0473 211028)
Surrey: The Rev'd David Eaton, The Vicarage, Rowledge, Farnham, Surrey GU10 4EN (0252 125 2402)
Sussex: The Rev'd John Devereux, The Driveway, Shoreham-by-Sea, Sussex (07917 4093)
Thames Valley: The Rev'd Canon Alan Christmas, 26 Lansdowne Avenue, Slough SL1 3SJ (0753 30230)
Tyne and Wear: Mr. Eric Dodgson, 17 Longridge Drive, Monkseaton, Whitley Bay NE26 3EN (091 252 6873)
Wakefield: The Rev'd Hugh Meiningen, Service House, 11 York Street, Wakefield, West Yorkshire WF1 3LQ (0924 377015)
Worcestershire: The Rev'd Michael Herbert, The Vicarage, Church

Road, Webheath, Redditch, Worcester WR5 2BW (0905 402404)
Edinburgh: The Rev'd Donald Ross, Industrial Mission Office, 121 George Street, Edinburgh EH2 4YN (031 225 5722)
Glasgow: The Rev'd Norman Orr, Industrial Mission Office, 59 Elmbank Street, Glasgow G2 4PY (041 332 4458)
Cardiff: The Rev'd Douglas Bale, 55 Duffryn Avenue, Cynoed, Cardiff CF2 6JL (0222 753139)
Newport: The Rev'd Ray Taylor, 28 Old Hill Crescent, Christchurch, Newport, Gwent NP6 1JN (0633 421017)
North East Wales: The Rev'd Michael Williams, The Vicarage, Whitford, Holywell, Clwyd CH8 9AJ (0745 560489)

Names and Addresses of Helpful Organisations
Government Departments

Council for Small Industries in Rural Areas
141 Castle Street,
Salisbury,
Wiltshire, SP1 3TP
Telephone 0722 336255
Grants and training for business operating and starting up in rural areas

Department of Health and Social Security
Alexander Fleming House,
Elephant and Castle,
London, SE1 6BY
Telephone 01 407 5522
Grants under the Opportunities for Volunteering Schemes

Department of the Environment
Urban Programme,
2 Marsham Street,
London, SW1P 3EB
Telephone 01 212 3434
Urban Grants

Department of Trade and Industry
1 Victoria Street,
London, SW1 0ET
Telephone 01 212 7676
Small Business Loan Guarantee Scheme, Business Expansion Scheme, Small Firms Information and Counselling Service

Information Technology Consultancy Unit
Information Technology Centre,
Consultancy Unit,
189 Freston Road,
London, W10 6TH
Telephone 01 969 8942
Help and advice for ITECS

Manpower Services Commission (Head Office)
Moorfoot,
Sheffield, S1 4PQ
Telephone 0742 704317
Grants, help and advice for CP, VPP, YTS, ITECS

National Youth Bureau
17–23 Albion Street,
Leicester, LE1 6GD
Telephone 0533 554775
*Training, information and all aspects
of Youth Unemployment*

The Department of Employment
Caxton House,
Tothill Street,
London, SW1H 9NF
Telephone 01 213 3000
YWS and Job Sharing Schemes

The Home Office
Voluntary Services Unit,
Queen Anne's Gate,
London, SW1
Telephone 01 213 6398
Assists the Voluntary Sector

Independent
Organisations

Action Resource Centre
Henrietta House,
9 Henrietta Place,
London, W1M 9AG
Telephone 01 629 3826

Scottish Action Resource Centre
54 Shandwick Place,
Edinburgh, EH2 4RT
Telephone 031 226 3669
and
4 Blythswood Square,
Glasgow, G2 4AB
Telephone 041 226 3639
*Secondment of skills from businesses
to groups who need the expertise*

British Unemployment Resource
Network
Birmingham Settlement,
318 Summer Lane,
Birmingham, B19 6RL
Telephone 021 359 3562
*Assists and develops self-help
initiatives*

Business in the Community
227A City Road,
London, EC1V 1JU
Telephone 01 253 3716

Scottish Business in the Community
Eagle Star House,
25 St. Andrew Square,
Edinburgh, EH2 1AF
Telephone 031 556 9761
*Help and advice for new and young
enterprises*

Community Industry
24 Highbury Crescent,
London, N5 1RX
Telephone 01 226 6663
*Organised to provide mainly manual
and construction jobs on projects
with local authorities and voluntary
organisations*

Community Projects Foundation
(CPF)
60 Highbury Grove,
London, N5 2AG
Telephone 01 226 5375
*Advice to sponsors of MSC
programmes*

Community Service Volunteers
237 Pentonville Road,
London, N1 9NJ
Telephone 01 278 2390

Northern Ireland Office
2nd/3rd Floor,
22 High Street,
Belfast, BT1 2BD
Telephone 0232 246981

Scottish Office
90 West Nile Street,
Glasgow, G1 2QH
Telephone 041 331 2375

Welsh Office
3rd Floor,
23 St. Mary Street,
Cardiff, CF1 2AA
Telephone 0222 388224
*Offers young people the chance to
help tackle social problems*

Community Task Force
Lowthian House,
Preston, PR1 2ES
Telephone 0772 51878
*Largest National Sponsor of MSC
special programmes*

Cooperative Development Agency
Broadmead House,
21 Panton Street,
London, SW1Y 4DR
Telephone 01 839 2985

Belfast Office
30 Adelaide Park,
Belfast, BT9 6FY
Telephone 0232 665368
*Provides links with local co-operative
development agencies*

Cooperatives Research Unit
The Open University,
Technology Faculty,
Walton Hall,
Milton Keynes, MK7 6AA
Telephone 0908 652102
*Information and research on co-
operatives*

Education for Enterprise Network
National Extension College,
Brooklands Avenue,
Cambridge, CB2 2HN
Telephone 0223 316644
*Provides intelligence, information
and courses to help stimulate self
employment*

Industrial Common Ownership
Finance Ltd.
4 St. Giles Street,
Northampton, NN1 1AA
Telephone 0604 37563
Provides grants for co-operatives

Industrial Common Ownership
Movement
7/8 The Corn Exchange,
Leeds, LS1 7BP
Telephone 0532 461737
Assists and advises co-operatives

Instant Muscle
c/o Rank Xerox UK Ltd.,
Cambridge House,
Oxford Road,
Uxbridge, UB8 1HS
Telephone 0895 51133
*Helps young people become self-
employed*

Inter-Action Trust
15 Wilkin Street,
London, NW5 3NG
Telephone 01 267 9421
*Helps with problem solving and
training the voluntary sector*

International Business Centre
50 Dornley Street,
Glasgow, G41
Telephone 041 429 2144

Job Ownership Ltd.
9 Poland Street,
London, W1V 3DG
Telephone 01 437 5511
*Consultancy and encouragement of
worker owned businesses*

Livewire England and Wales
National Extension College,
18 Brooklands Avenue,
Cambridge, CB2 2HN
Telephone 0223 316644
*Helps the 16–25 year olds work for
themselves with grants and advice*

Local Economic Development
Information Service,
186 Bath Street,
Glasgow, G2 4HG
Telephone 041 332 8541
Advice

Mutual Aid Centre Managing
Agency
The Georgian House,
28 Lower Clapton Road,
London, E5 0PD
Telephone 01 986 4411
*Helps to plan and support volunteer
organisations wishing to participate
in MSC special programmes*

Mutual Support Network Wales
78 Bridge Street,
Newport,
Gwent, NP7 4AC
Telephone 0633 59947
Assists those involved in self-help groups

National Council for Voluntary Organisations
26 Bedford Square,
London, WC1B 3HU
Telephone 01 636 4066
Information and advice

Neighbourhood Energy Action
2–4 Bigg Market,
Newcastle upon Tyne, NE1 1UW
Telephone 0632 615677
Helps to employ people on neighbourhood energy programmes

New Ways to Work
347A Upper Street,
London, N1 0PD
Telephone 01 226 4026
Information on job sharing

Practical Action
Victoria Chambers,
16–20 Strutton Ground,
London, SW1P 2HP
Telephone 01 222 3341

86 Lisburn Road,
Belfast, BT9 6AF
Telephone 0232 681447
Acts as a broker between business and the community helping with equipment

Project Fullemploy
Robert Hyde House,
48 Bryanston Square,
London, W1H 7LN
Telephone 01 262 2405
Major operator of training centres primarily with MSC and business sponsorship

Project North East
5 Saville Place,
Newcastle upon Tyne, NE1 8DQ
Telephone 0632 617856
Assists with self-employment

Retired Executives Action Clearing House
Victoria House,
Southampton Row,
London, WC1B 4DH
Telephone 01 404 0940
Brings older peoples' skills to work in the community: especially for groups who need but cannot afford the help

Scottish Cooperatives Development Committee
Templeton Business Centre,
Templeton Street,
Bridgeton,
Glasgow, G40 1DA
Telephone 041 554 3797
Helps, promotes and provides local links with agencies for co-operatives

The Centre for Employment Initiatives
140A Gloucester Mansions,
Cambridge Circus,
London, WC2H 8PA
Telephone 01 240 8901

and

361 Royal Liver Building,
Pier Head,
Liverpool, L3 1JH
Telephone 051 236 6360
Assists all bodies to respond to the unemployment situation

The Royal Jubilee and Prince's Trusts
Youth Business Initiative,
8 Buckingham Street,
London, WC2N 6BU
Telephone 01 930 9811
Provides bursaries for the under 25s to help self-employment

The Unemployment Project
Community Education,
The Open University,
Walton Hall,
Milton Keynes, MK7 6AA
Telephone 0908 652168
*Offers learning materials specially
designed for the unemployed*

The Volunteer Centre
29 Lower King's Road,
Berkamstead, Herts, HP4 2AB
Telephone 04427 73311
*Promotes and advises charitable and
voluntary organisations*

Urban and Economic Development
UBBED, 99 Southwark Street,
London, SE1 0JF
Telephone 01 928 9515
*Information, advice and technical
assistance*

Volunteer Development Scotland
18–19 Claremont Crescent,
Edinburgh, EH7 4QD
Telephone 031 556 3882
Promotes volunteering in Scotland

Wales Cooperative Development
and Training Centre Ltd.
Llandaff Court, Fairwater Road,
Llandaff, Cardiff,
South Glamorgan, CF5 2XP
Telephone 0222 554965
and
Morfa Hall, Church Street,
Rhyl, Clwydd, LL18 3AA
Telephone 0745 55336
*Encourages and offers expertise for
co-operatives*

Welsh Authorities

Executive Secondment Ltd.
Treforest Industrial Estate,
Pontypridd,
Mid Glamorgan, CF37 5UT
Telephone 044 385 2666
*Provides senior executive help to
small businesses*

Mid Wales Development
Development Board for Rural
Wales,
Ladywell House,
Newtown,
Powys, SY16 1JB
Telephone 0686 26965
*Grants and advice for rural business
development*

Wales Council for Voluntary Action
Llys Ifor,
Crescent Road,
Caerphilly, CF8 1XL
Telephone 0222 869111
and
North Wales Office
57A King Street,
Wrexham,
Clwydd
Telephone 0978 261245
*Provides training and advice for
voluntary organisations wishing to
operate MSC special programmes*

Welsh Development Agency
P.O. Box 100,
Greyfriars Road,
Cardiff, CF1 1WF
Telephone 0222 32955
*Grants and advice for people who
will develop employment and
industry in Wales*

Scottish Authorities

Community Business Scotland
Central,
39 Vicar Street,
Falkirk, FK1 1LL
Telephone 0324 38458

Lothian
Livingston Development
Corporation
Lammermuir House,
Gwen Square,
Livingston
Telephone 0506 413188

Local Enterprise Advisory Project
Westerfield Annexe,
25 High Calside,
Paisley, Renfrewshire
Telephone 041 8871241
*Helps develop and support
community businesses among the
unemployed*

Highlands and Islands Development
Board
Bridge House, 27 Bank Street,
Inverness, IV1 1QR
Telephone 0463 234171
*Grants for the development of
business in the Highlands and Islands
of Scotland*

Scottish Community Education
Council
Atholl House, 2 Canning Street,
Edinburgh, EH3 8EG
Telephone 031 229 2433
An unemployment initiative service

Scottish Council of Social Service
19 Claremont Crescent,
Edinburgh, EH7 4QD
Telephone 031 556 3882
*Promotes voluntary organisations
and manages a large CP project*

Scottish Development Agency
Small Business Division,
Roseberry House,
Haymarket Terrace,
Edinburgh, EH12 5EZ
Telephone 031 337 9595
*Help, advice and grants for new
businesses, urban projects and youth
enterprise schemes*

Northern Irish Authorities

Community Projects Branch
Howard House,
1 Brunswick Street,
Belfast, BT2 7GE
Telephone 0232 244377
*Comparable with the MSC
community and voluntary special
employment schemes*

Cooperative Education Research
and Training Unit
New University of Ulster,
Magee University College,
Londonderry
Telephone 0504 265621
Training courses for co-operatives

Department of Economic
Development
Grants to Employers Branch,
IDB House,
64 Chichester Street,
Belfast, BT1 4PS
Telephone 0232 234488
*YWS, YTP, Job Splitting, key
worker and training schemes*

Department of the Environment for
Northern Ireland
Clarendon House,
Adelaide Street,
Belfast, BT2 8ND
Telephone 0232 244300
Urban development grants

Local Enterprise Development Unit
Lamont House,
Purdy's Lane,
Newtownbreda,
Belfast, BT8 4AR
Telephone 0232 691031
*Grants for existing businesses that
will result in increased employment,
together with expert help*

Northern Ireland Council of Social
Services
2 Anandale Avenue,
Belfast, BT7 3JH
Telephone 0232 640011
*Help and advice for voluntary
agencies*

Northern Ireland Small Business
Institute
c/o Ulster Polytechnic,
Jordanstown,
Newtonabbey,
Co. Antrim
Telephone Jordanstown 65131
*Training, information and help to
encourage small businesses*

Northern Ireland Voluntary Trust
Howard House,
1 Brunswick Street,
Belfast, BT2 7GE
Telephone 0232 245927
*Small grants for employment
initiatives in Northern Ireland*

Youth Training Programme
Netherleigh,
Massey Avenue,
Belfast, BT4 2BS
Telephone 0232 63244
Equivalent to MSC, YTS